A SAINSBURY COOKBOOK

WHOLEFOOD COOKERY FOR EVERYONE

GAIL DUFF

CONTENTS

Published exclusively for J Sainsbury plc
Stamford House Stamford Street
London SE1 9LL
by Woodhead-Faulkner (Publishers) Ltd
Fitzwilliam House 32 Trumpington Street
Cambridge CB2 1QY

First published 1986

Printed in Great Britain

THE AUTHOR

Gail Duff was born in Aylesbury, Bucks but has spent most of her teenage and adult life in Kent. Gail was attracted by food and cookery from an early age, and this eventually led her to become involved in demonstrating, broadcasting and writing about the subjects which interested her. She has always been enthusiastic about natural foods and is well known for her range of books on vegetarian and wholefood cookery. Her most popular books include: *Gail Duff's Vegetarian Cookbook; Good Housekeeping Wholefood Cookery; Good Healthy Food; Real Fast Food* and *The Barbecue Cookbook*. She has also written a Food Guide for Sainsbury's called *Rice and Pulses*.

Gail now lives near Maidstone with her husband, who is a photographer, and small daughter.

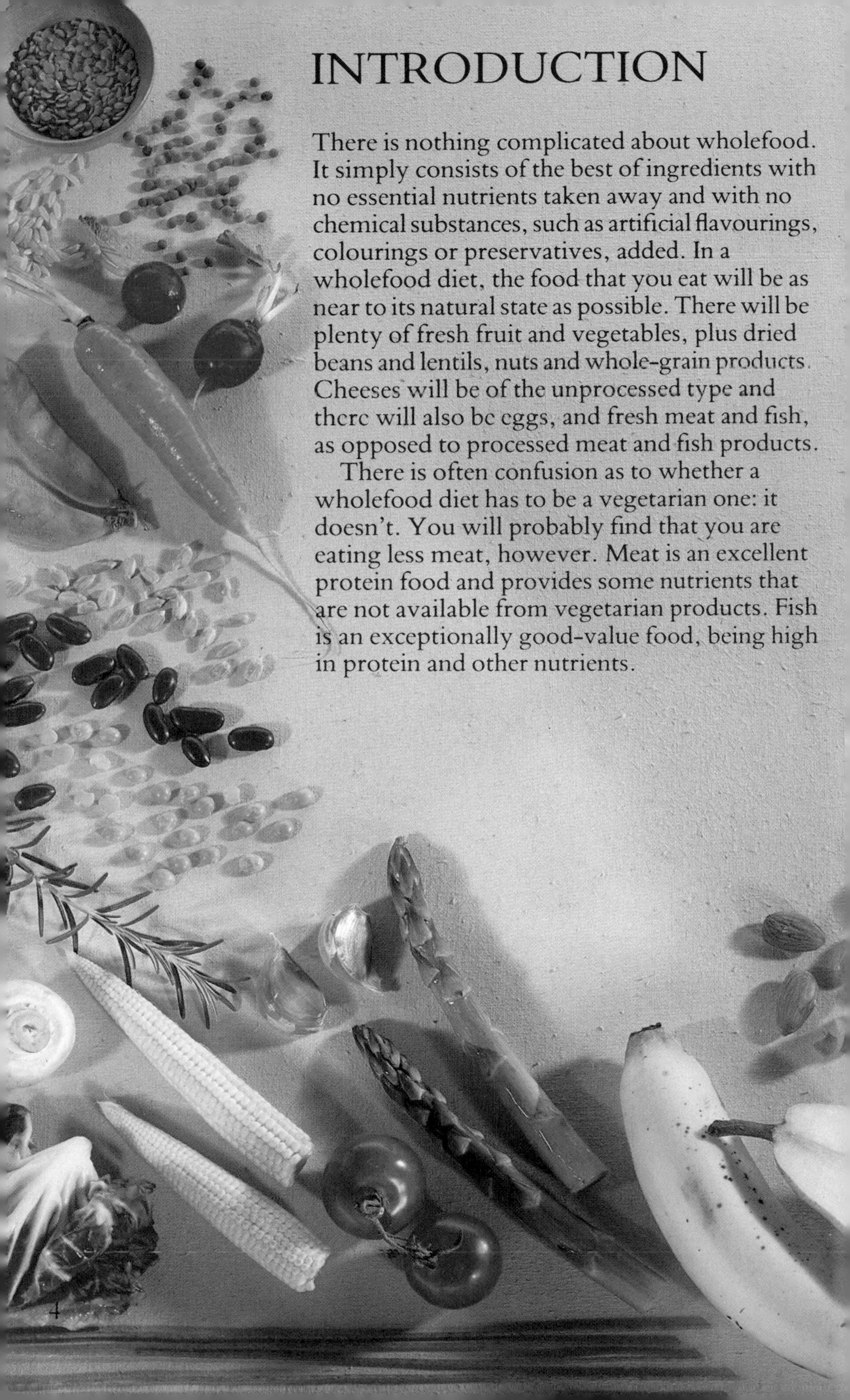

INTRODUCTION

There is nothing complicated about wholefood. It simply consists of the best of ingredients with no essential nutrients taken away and with no chemical substances, such as artificial flavourings, colourings or preservatives, added. In a wholefood diet, the food that you eat will be as near to its natural state as possible. There will be plenty of fresh fruit and vegetables, plus dried beans and lentils, nuts and whole-grain products. Cheeses will be of the unprocessed type and there will also be eggs, and fresh meat and fish, as opposed to processed meat and fish products.

There is often confusion as to whether a wholefood diet has to be a vegetarian one: it doesn't. You will probably find that you are eating less meat, however. Meat is an excellent protein food and provides some nutrients that are not available from vegetarian products. Fish is an exceptionally good-value food, being high in protein and other nutrients.

A much more talked-about constituent of our diet is fibre, and a wholefood diet is naturally high in fibre. Many people interested in natural foods have been saying it for years, but medical experts have recently confirmed that fibre in a diet is essential for the health of our digestive systems and probably for other aspects of our well-being as well. Fresh fruit and vegetables, pulses and whole grains are all fibre-rich foods and these will appear frequently in your daily menus. Eat well, and there will be no need to sprinkle bran on your food!

A wholefood diet will, on the other hand, be naturally low in fat. Much has been said on the subject of fats and much more research has to be done. What has emerged from recent findings is that, probably, we are all eating too much. Changing to a wholefood diet will automatically help you to cut down on your fat consumption, however, and reduce the proportion of saturated fats in what you eat. The meat in your diet should be lean, and some meat meals will be replaced with those made from pulses, nuts and whole grains.

Wholefoods contain little or no added sugar, and this is another of their advantages compared with processed foods. Sugar is high in calories but has little nutritional value. The energy it releases into the bloodstream is used up very quickly, causing a craving for yet more sugar, and this vicious circle can lead to obesity. A wholefood diet releases energy more steadily into the bloodstream, and so helps to regulate appetite. In fact, sufferers from diabetes are recommended to increase their consumption of wholefoods, for this reason. Where sugar is necessary, Barbados (also known as muscovado) and molasses sugars, which contain small amounts of minerals and vitamins, are preferred. People with a sweet tooth will find that wholefood cakes and biscuits are just as delicious and tempting as the ones they are used to, and will enjoy the wide range of wholefood snacks, such as muesli bars, now on sale.

If you are eating more wholefoods, you will also automatically cut down your intake of salt, which is added to many processed foods but is considered by some authorities to contribute to high blood-pressure. You will also find that fresh ingredients have a better flavour than processed ones and do not need to be improved with extra seasoning. In this book, herbs and spices feature prominently as flavourings, as do cooking methods which preserve flavour and texture, so that fresh foods really come into their own.

All recent research has found that we should all be thinking more about our diet, both as an insurance policy for our future health and for our present state of well-being. Wholefood is not an overnight cure for all ills, but after gradually switching to a more natural diet over a few months many people find that they generally feel better, perhaps with fewer minor illnesses, and reach and maintain a more normal weight. A true wholefood diet will provide a wide range of nutrients with sufficient calories to see us through the day with energy and enthusiasm, but not too many to be stored as fat.

Everyone can enjoy a wholefood diet.

Although small children have special dietary needs which should always be discussed with your doctor or health visitor, you can give them the foundations of healthy eating patterns for the rest of their lives. School children will be active and healthy, working parents will have enough energy for both home and work and pensioners can enjoy a more comfortable retirement.

Wholefood eating is not expensive. Out of the shopping basket will go all the processed products and also some meat meals will be replaced with pulses. Admittedly, some of the products you will be using, such as brown rice and wholewheat pasta, are more expensive than their refined counterparts, but, when each side is weighed up, you will certainly break even and may quite well save a little.

Even a household of two people or one person living alone can enjoy wholefoods. Many of the recipes in this book can be easily cut down and special instructions are given for doing this where necessary.

If you have never thought about a wholefood diet before, make the change gradually. A sudden, complete change could be a shock to the system. Start first by simply changing wholemeal bread for white and using brown rice and wholewheat pasta instead of the white equivalents. Whenever you bake, or make pastry, use wholemeal flour. After this, take a look along the supermarket shelves at the tempting arrays of fresh vegetables. Try to eat fresh vegetables twice a day: once prepared as a salad and once cooked with a hot main dish.

You are already half-way there! If you have never eaten pulses before, buy a packet and try them using some of the recipes in this book. There are all kinds of different varieties, so buy a packet a week and experiment with them. Then look at all the different types of grains there are to go with them.

Very soon, you will find that the contents of your store-cupboard have changed and you will be feeling much better for it.

Note on quantities
All recipes in this book give ingredients in both metric (g, ml, etc.) and imperial (oz, pints, etc.) measures. Use either set of quantities, but not both, in any one recipe. All teaspoons and tablespoons are level unless otherwise stated. Egg size is medium (size 3) unless otherwise stated. Preparation and cooking times are given as a guideline: all timings are approximate.

A Day's Healthy Eating

Breakfast:
Muesli with fresh fruit; or boiled or poached egg with wholemeal toast or bread; or yogurt with fresh fruits and/or whole-grain cereal; or grilled tomatoes on wholemeal toast.
Lunch:
A large, mixed salad with as many fresh vegetables as you can find, yogurt or oil and vinegar dressing, wholemeal bread or crispbreads. Low-fat cheese, a few cooked beans or chopped nuts can be added. Fresh fruit or dried fruit or muesli bar if you want.
Dinner:
Any main dish from the recipes below, with two different types of vegetable plus a jacket potato or a whole grain. Have either a first course or soup or a dessert.

SOUPS FOR ALL OCCASIONS

CHICKEN STOCK

Preparation time: 20 minutes + 1½ hours cooking

- *1 small chicken portion or 250 g (8 oz) chicken giblets*
- *1 large carrot, chopped roughly*
- *2 sticks of celery, chopped roughly*
- *1 large onion, unpeeled, halved*
- *2.3 litres (4 pints) water*
- *a bouquet garni sachet*
- *1 teaspoon black peppercorns*

Put the chicken portion or giblets into a large saucepan with the carrot, celery and onion. No fat is necessary. Set them on a low heat for 10 minutes, turning once, so the chicken begins to brown.

Pour in the water and bring it to the boil. Add the bouquet garni and peppercorns. Simmer, uncovered, for 1½ hours. Cool the stock and strain it. Store in a covered container in the refrigerator for up to 5 days.

Note: if you can buy beef marrow bones, you can use these very successfully instead of the chicken.

VEGETABLE STOCK

Preparation time: 10 minutes + 45 minutes cooking

- *2 carrots*
- *3 sticks of celery*
- *1 large onion, halved, unpeeled*
- *1 small potato, scrubbed and halved*
- *trimmings from other vegetables such as outer leaves of cabbages, stalks of spring greens, outer parts of runner beans, bean and pea pods, in about same quantity as other vegetables*
- *a bouquet garni sachet*
- *1 teaspoon black peppercorns*
- *2.3 litres (4 pints) water*

Put all the ingredients into a large saucepan and bring them to the boil. Simmer, uncovered, for 45 minutes. Cool, strain and store as above.

CURRIED CAULIFLOWER SOUP

Basic recipe: Vegetable Stock (page 9) Serves 4

Preparation time: 30 minutes + 20 minutes cooking

1 medium-size cauliflower

1 medium-size onion, chopped finely

600 ml (1 pint) vegetable stock

a bouquet garni sachet

25 g (1 oz) butter or vegetable margarine

1 tablespoon wholemeal flour

1 teaspoon hot Madras curry powder

450 g (15 oz) carton of natural yogurt

sea salt and freshly ground black pepper

To garnish:

2 tablespoons flaked almonds, toasted

Natural yogurt gives this soup a delightful fresh taste which goes well with the mild curry flavour. The almond garnish is not essential, but it turns the soup from an everyday recipe into one that is rather special.

Break the cauliflower into small florets and put these into a saucepan with the onion, stock and bouquet garni. Season, bring to the boil, cover, and simmer for 15 minutes.

Remove the bouquet garni and either work the soup in a blender or food processor or put it through the fine blade of a vegetable mill.

Melt the butter or margarine in a saucepan on a medium heat. Stir in the flour and curry powder and cook them for 1 minute. Stir in the blended cauliflower mixture and bring it to the boil, stirring. Simmer for 2 minutes.

Take the pan from the heat and stir in the yogurt just before serving. Do not let it boil after you have added the yogurt.

Serve in individual bowls, garnished with the toasted flaked almonds.

BEEF AND BEAN MINESTRONE

Basic recipe: Chicken Stock (page 9) Serves 4

Preparation time: 20 minutes + soaking overnight + 1½ hours cooking

125 g (4 oz) haricot beans, soaked overnight

1 tablespoon sunflower oil

250 g (8 oz) lean minced beef

1 red pepper, de-seeded and chopped finely

1 green pepper, de-seeded and chopped finely

350 g (12 oz) courgettes, sliced thinly

2 medium-size onions, chopped finely

1 clove of garlic, chopped finely

1.2 litres (2 pints) chicken stock

2 tablespoons tomato purée

75 g (3 oz) wholewheat spaghetti, broken into small pieces

4 tablespoons chopped fresh parsley

1 tablespoon chopped fresh thyme or 1 teaspoon dried thyme

1 tablespoon chopped fresh marjoram or 1 teaspoon dried marjoram

This is a soup for a main course. It is a high-fibre soup that enables a little beef to go a long way.

Drain and rinse the soaked beans, and bring them to the boil in fresh water. Boil for 10 minutes and then simmer them for 50 minutes. Drain again. Heat the oil in a large, heavy saucepan on a high heat. Put in the beef and stir it until it browns. Put in the peppers, courgettes, onions and garlic. Lower the heat and cook, stirring frequently, for 5 minutes.

Pour in the stock and bring it to the boil. Add the tomato purée, beans, spaghetti and herbs. Cover, and simmer for 30 minutes.

Serve in big, deep bowls and accompany it with wholemeal bread.

TOMATO AND LENTIL SOUP

Basic recipe: Vegetable Stock (page 9) Serves 4

Preparation time: 15 minutes + 45 minutes cooking

750 g (1½ lb) ripe tomatoes
3 tablespoons sunflower oil
1 large onion, chopped finely
1 clove of garlic, chopped finely
125 g (4 oz) split red lentils
2 tablespoons chopped fresh parsley
1 tablespoon chopped fresh thyme or 1 teaspoon dried thyme
1 tablespoon chopped fresh marjoram or 1 teaspoon dried marjoram
600 ml (1 pint) vegetable stock
a pinch of sea salt
freshly ground black pepper
To garnish:
4 tablespoons natural yogurt

Split red lentils give flavour and body to any soup. The simple combination of ingredients in this deep orange tomato soup brings out all the natural flavours.

Scald, skin and chop the tomatoes. Heat the oil in a saucepan on a low heat. Put in the onion and garlic and soften them. Put in the tomatoes, lentils and herbs. Stir for 2 minutes or until the tomatoes are soft. Mash them down with a fork or potato masher.

Pour in the stock, bring it to the boil and season. Cover the pan and simmer for 45 minutes or until the lentils are soft.

Serve in individual bowls with the yogurt spooned or swirled over the top, depending on its texture.

Beef and Bean Minestrone
Tomato and Lentil Soup

THICK VEGETABLE SOUP

Basic recipe: Vegetable Stock (page 9) Serves 4

Preparation time: 15 minutes + 20 minutes cooking

25 g (1 oz) butter or vegetable margarine

250 g (8 oz) carrots, diced

250 g (8 oz) parsnips, diced

125 g (4 oz) swede, diced

125 g (4 oz) potato, peeled and diced

1 medium-size onion, chopped finely

900 ml (1½ pints) vegetable stock

2 tablespoons chopped fresh parsley

freshly ground black pepper

This is a warming winter soup with a delicious creamy texture.

Melt the butter or margarine in a saucepan on a low heat. Stir in the vegetables. Cover and allow them to sweat for 5 minutes. Pour in the stock and bring it to the boil. Season with the pepper. Cover, and simmer for 20 minutes.

Liquidise half the soup in a blender or food processor. Stir it back into the rest. Add the parsley and reheat before serving.

LEEK, OATMEAL AND BACON SOUP

Basic recipe: Chicken Stock (page 9) Serves 4

Preparation time: 10 minutes + 20 minutes cooking

250 g (8 oz) lean back bacon, de-rinded and chopped finely

50 g (2 oz) porridge oats

2 teaspoons mustard powder

900 ml (1½ pints) chicken stock

750 g (1½ lb) leeks, washed and sliced finely

6 fresh sage leaves, chopped, or 1 teaspoon dried sage

Oatmeal thickens and enriches soups deliciously. This soup is best served before a light meal or even as a lunch or supper dish by itself.

Put the bacon into a saucepan and set it on a low heat until it is cooked through but not browned. Add the oats and cook, stirring, for half a minute. Stir in the mustard powder. Pour in the stock and bring it to the boil. Put in the leeks and sage and bring to the boil again. Cover, and simmer for 20 minutes after which it is ready to serve.

MUSHROOM AND GREEN PEPPER SOUP

Basic recipe: Vegetable Stock (page 9) Serves 4

Preparation time: 15 minutes + 20 minutes cooking

3 tablespoons sunflower oil

250 g (8 oz) dark, flat mushrooms, chopped finely

1 large onion, chopped finely

2 tablespoons wholemeal flour

900 ml (1½ pints) vegetable stock

1 bay leaf

2 teaspoons chopped fresh thyme or ½ teaspoon dried thyme

1 green pepper, de-seeded and chopped

4 tablespoons chopped fresh parsley

freshly ground black pepper

This soup is easy to make as it requires no blending or sieving. The richness of the mushrooms and the bitter-sweet flavour of the pepper go particularly well together.

Heat the oil in a saucepan on a low heat. Stir in the mushrooms and onion. Cover and cook gently for 10 minutes. Stir in the flour and then the stock. Bring to the boil, stirring. Add the bay leaf and thyme and season with the black pepper. Simmer, uncovered, for 15 minutes. Add the green pepper and cook for a further 5 minutes. Remove the bay leaf and add the parsley before serving.

Note: for a special occasion, use only 750 ml (1¼ pints) of stock. Then add 150 ml (¼ pint) dry sherry with the parsley and reheat if necessary, without boiling.

CHILLED AVOCADO SOUP

Preparation time: 10 minutes + 2 hours chilling Serves 4

2 ripe avocados

500 g (1 lb 2 oz) carton of natural fromage frais or other skimmed milk soft cheese

900 ml (1½ pints) tomato juice

1 clove of garlic, crushed

This soup could not be easier to make. It has a creamy texture and is perfect for a summer evening.

Peel and stone the avocados and chop them. Put them, in 2 or 3 batches, into a blender or food processor with the cheese, tomato juice and garlic and work to a smooth soup.

Alternatively, rub the avocados, garlic and cheese through a sieve and then stir in the tomato juice gradually.

Chill the soup for 2 hours before serving.

SPICY CARROT SOUP

Basic recipe: Vegetable Stock (page 9) Serves 4

Preparation time: 30 minutes + 20 minutes cooking

500 g (1 lb) carrots, scraped
15 g (½ oz) butter or vegetable margarine
1 medium-size onion, sliced thinly
1 clove of garlic, chopped finely
1 teaspoon paprika
a good pinch of chilli powder
900 ml (1½ pints) vegetable stock
1 tablespoon tomato purée

This is a warming soup which relies only on the carrots themselves for its thick texture. The grated carrot garnish makes a fresh contrast, in texture and appearance.

Finely grate 50 g (2 oz) of the carrots. Thinly slice the rest. Melt the butter or margarine in a saucepan on a low heat. Stir in the sliced carrots, onion, garlic, paprika and chilli powder. Cover the pan and cook on a very low heat for 10 minutes. Pour in the stock and add the tomato purée. Bring the soup to the boil, cover, and simmer for 20 minutes.

Either work the soup in a blender or food processor or put it through the fine blade of a vegetable mill. Return it to the saucepan and reheat if necessary. Serve in individual bowls, with the grated carrot floating on top.

Pigeon and Vegetable Soup
Chilled Broad Bean and Pea Soup
Spicy Carrot Soup

CHILLED BROAD BEAN AND PEA SOUP

Basic recipe: Vegetable Stock (page 9) Serves 4

Preparation time: 10 minutes + 20 minutes cooking + 2 hours chilling

1 kg (2 lb) broad beans in pods, or 350 g (12 oz) frozen broad beans, thawed

500 g (1 lb) peas in pods, or 250 g (8 oz) frozen peas, thawed

25 g (1 oz) vegetable margarine

1 large onion, chopped finely

900 ml (1½ pints) vegetable stock

2 sprigs of mint

150 g (5.29 oz) carton of natural yogurt

¼ teaspoon curry paste

To garnish:

2 tablespoons chopped fresh mint

This soup can be made with either fresh or frozen beans and peas. It has a thick, creamy texture and a flavour that is lightened by the yogurt.

Shell the beans and peas if they are fresh. Melt the margarine in a saucepan on a low heat. Mix in the onion and soften it. Pour in the stock and bring it to the boil. Put in the beans, peas and mint sprigs. Cover, and simmer for 20 minutes.

Remove the mint sprigs. Work the rest in a blender or food processor to a smooth, green purée. Beat the yogurt with the curry paste. Add these to the soup and blend it again.

Chill the soup for 2 hours. Serve in individual bowls with the chopped mint scattered over the top.

PIGEON AND VEGETABLE SOUP

Basic recipe: Chicken Stock (page 9) Serves 4

Preparation time: 20 minutes + 1½ hours cooking

2 large carrots, sliced

1 large white turnip, diced

1 medium-size parsnip, diced

250 g (8 oz) leeks, sliced

4 large sticks of celery, sliced

1 medium-size onion, chopped

15 g (½ oz) butter or vegetable margarine

1 wood pigeon

2 tablespoons wholemeal flour

½ teaspoon ground mace

½ a nutmeg, grated, or ½ teaspoon ground nutmeg

1.5 litres (2½ pints) chicken stock

juice of ½ a lemon

a bouquet garni sachet

To garnish:

4 tablespoons chopped fresh parsley

This is another main-meal soup which makes an economical use of game and winter vegetables.

Prepare all the vegetables. Melt the butter or margarine in a large saucepan on a high heat. Put in the pigeon and brown it all over. Remove it and lower the heat. Mix in the vegetables, cover them and cook them gently for 5 minutes. Stir in the flour, mace and nutmeg and cook for 1 minute. Stir in the stock and bring it to the boil. Replace the pigeon. Add the lemon juice and bouquet garni, cover, and simmer for 1½ hours.

Take out the pigeon. Cut away all the meat and dice it finely. Return it to the soup and reheat if necessary. Ladle the soup into deep bowls or a tureen and scatter the parsley over the top.

Note: you can add the diced vegetables half-way through the cooking time, without pre-softening them, if you prefer them with a firmer texture.

FIRST COURSES AND LIGHT LUNCHES

ORANGE AND TUNA SALAD

Preparation time: 15 minutes | Serves 4

2 medium-size oranges
99 g (3½ oz) can of tuna fish
125 g (4 oz) curd cheese
2 tablespoons natural yogurt
1 tablespoon chopped capers
1 tablespoon chopped fresh parsley
4 black olives

Mix tuna fish and curd cheese and you have a simply-made pâté, which looks attractive and tastes good with sliced orange and the sharp taste of olives.

Cut the rind and pith from the oranges and cut each orange into four slices. Arrange them on four small plates.

Drain and flake the tuna. Beat the cheese with the yogurt. Mix in the capers, parsley and tuna. Put a spoonful or so of the mixture on top of each orange slice and top each with an olive.

CELERY AND SUNFLOWER SALAD WITH BANANA DRESSING

Preparation time: 20 minutes | Serves 4

2 ripe bananas
4 tablespoons cider vinegar
1 clove of garlic, crushed
6 sticks of celery
50 g (2 oz) sunflower seeds or melon seeds
50 g (2 oz) sultanas
freshly ground black pepper

Bananas mixed with cider vinegar make a low-calorie, sweet-and-sour dressing which will complement a salad of celery, crunchy seeds and dried fruit.

Mash the bananas and work in the vinegar, garlic and pepper. This will make the dressing. Slice the celery. Divide the salad between four small bowls. Pour on the dressing and sprinkle the sunflower or melon seeds and sultanas over the top.

Celery and Sunflower Salad with Banana Dressing
Orange and Tuna Salad

PASTA WITH CELERY, APPLE AND WALNUTS

Preparation time: 25 minutes — Serves 4

250 g (8 oz) wholewheat pasta shells, spirals, rings or cut macaroni

25 g (1 oz) butter or vegetable margarine

6 sticks of celery, chopped finely

1 medium-size onion, chopped finely

1 large cooking apple, chopped finely

75 g (3 oz) walnuts, chopped

75 g (3 oz) Red Leicester cheese, grated

2 tablespoons Worcestershire sauce

4 tablespoons chopped fresh parsley

The celery mixture in this recipe can be prepared while the pasta is cooking, making your cooking and preparation time very short. Once mixed with the sauce, the pasta can be cooled and reheated later. No accompaniment is needed.

Cook the pasta in lightly salted boiling water for 12 minutes or until it is just tender. Drain it, run cold water through it and drain it again.

Melt the butter or margarine in a saucepan on a low heat. Put in the celery and onion and cook them for 2 minutes. Put in the apple and cook until the celery and onion are beginning to brown. Mix in the pasta, walnuts, cheese and Worcestershire sauce. Divide the pasta between four bowls or plates and scatter some parsley over the top of each serving.

COURGETTES BAKED WITH CHEESE

Preparation time: 15 minutes + 30 minutes baking — Serves 4

500 g (1 lb) courgettes

oil for greasing

4 tablespoons chopped fresh parsley

75 g (3 oz) Farmhouse Cheddar cheese, or low-fat hard cheese, grated

Oven temperature:
Gas Mark 6/200°C/400°F

The courgettes in this dish should be just tender with the cheese melting into them without browning or bubbling. The parsley stays fresh and green. This makes an excellent lunch dish served with a jacket potato, as well as a first course.

Preheat the oven. Wipe and thinly slice the courgettes. Lay them in one large, greased, ovenproof dish or in four small ones. Scatter first the parsley and then the cheese over the top. Cover the dish with foil and put it into the oven for 30 minutes. Serve hot.

POTATOES FILLED WITH SWEETCORN

Preparation time: 15 minutes + 1½ hours cooking Serves 4

4 large potatoes

½ teaspoon yeast extract

4 tablespoons natural yogurt

1 tablespoon tomato purée

4 tablespoons chopped fresh parsley

326 g (11½ oz) can of sweetcorn, drained

50 g (2 oz) Edam cheese, grated (optional)

Oven temperature:
Gas Mark 6/200°C/400°F

Jacket potatoes are a popular snack meal. You can top them with cheese or sauces, or mix other ingredients into the scooped-out and mashed middles, returning them to the oven to brown. Salad, or simply some sliced tomatoes, would be a good accompaniment to this version.

Preheat the oven. Scrub the potatoes and prick each one on both sides with a fork. Lay them on the oven rack and bake them for 1 hour 15 minutes or until the outsides are crisp and the insides soft.

Cut each potato lengthways in half. Scoop the middles into a bowl. Beat in the yeast extract, yogurt, tomato purée and parsley. Mix the sweetcorn into the potato.

Pile the mixture back into the potato shells and put the shells in an ovenproof dish. If using the cheese, scatter it on top. Return the potatoes to the oven for 15 minutes, or until the cheese has melted, or the tops are beginning to brown.

AVOCADO WITH GRAPES AND YOGURT

Preparation time: 15 minutes Serves 4

2 ripe avocados

24 black grapes

150 g (5.29 oz) carton of natural yogurt

1 clove of garlic, crushed

2 tablespoons fresh chopped mint or parsley

freshly ground black pepper

Grapes and yogurt make a refreshing contrast to rich, creamy-textured avocado.

Cut the avocados in half and stone them. Put each avocado half into a small dish. Halve and de-seed the grapes. Put them into the centres of the avocados. Beat the yogurt with the garlic, pepper and mint or parsley. Spoon it over the top and serve immediately.

GREEN PEPPER TARTS

Basic recipe: Shortcrust Pastry (page 87) Serves 4–6

Preparation time: 20 minutes + about 30 minutes baking

3 tablespoons sunflower or olive oil

4 large green peppers, de-seeded and sliced

1 large onion, sliced thinly

1 clove of garlic, chopped finely

250 g (8 oz) fromage frais or other low-fat soft cheese

4 eggs, beaten

2 tablespoons chopped parsley

1 tablespoon chopped thyme or 1 teaspoon dried thyme

50 g (2 oz) salami, sliced thinly (optional)

shortcrust pastry made with 250 g (8 oz) wholemeal flour

Oven temperature:
Gas Mark 6/200°C/400°F

These savoury tarts can be eaten hot as a main meal or left to get cold for lunchtime snacks or for a buffet party.

Preheat the oven. Heat the oil in a frying pan on a low heat. Put in the peppers, onion and garlic and cook them until the onion is beginning to turn golden. Take them from the heat and allow them to cool.

Put the cheese into a bowl. Add the eggs, a little at a time, beating well. Beat in the parsley and thyme. Finely chop the salami and mix it into the cheese and eggs.

Roll out the pastry and line four patty tins or a 25 cm (10-inch) tart tin. Put in the peppers and onion and spread them out evenly. Pour in the cheese mixture. Bake the tarts for 30 minutes or until the filling is set and golden.

Green Pepper Tarts

French Bread filled with Cannellini Beans and Sardines

Tomato and Olive Pizza

FRENCH BREAD FILLED WITH CANNELLINI BEANS AND SARDINES

Preparation time: 15 minutes + 20 minutes baking | Serves 4

1 wholemeal french loaf

butter or vegetable margarine (optional)

3 tablespoons sunflower oil

1 large onion, sliced thinly

1 teaspoon paprika

¼ teaspoon chilli powder

400 g (14 oz) can of cannellini beans, drained

2 × 124 g (4 oz) can of sardines in oil, drained

juice of 1 lemon

4 tablespoons chopped fresh parsley

Oven temperature:
Gas Mark 6/200°C/400°F

French bread with some of the crumbs removed makes a good container for tasty fillings. Use the crumbs in a stuffing or nut dish on another occasion. Do not leave the foil parcels standing for longer than 10 minutes after they have come out of the oven, as the bread, which should be light and crisp, will become soggy.

Cut the french loaf into four equal-sized pieces. Slit them crossways almost all the way through. Remove most of the crumb, leaving shells about 1 cm (⅜-inch) thick. Spread them lightly with butter or margarine if you wish. Preheat the oven.

Heat the oil in a saucepan on a low heat. Stir in the onion, paprika and chilli powder and cook them gently until the onion is soft. Mix in the beans, sardines, lemon juice and parsley.

Fill the pieces of french bread with the beans and sardines. Wrap each piece individually in foil. Place the parcels on a baking sheet and bake them in the oven for 20 minutes.

TOMATO AND OLIVE PIZZA

Preparation time: 35 minutes + 25 minutes baking | Serves 4

For the base:

250 g (8 oz) wholemeal flour, plus extra for kneading

1 teaspoon fine sea salt

1 teaspoon bicarbonate of soda

3 tablespoons olive oil, plus extra for greasing

150 g (5.29 oz) carton of natural yogurt

For the topping:

500 g (1 lb) tomatoes

3 tablespoons olive oil

1 medium-size onion, chopped finely

1 clove of garlic, chopped finely

1 red pepper, de-seeded and chopped

1 green pepper, de-seeded and chopped

1 tablespoon chopped fresh thyme or 1 teaspoon dried thyme

1 tablespoon chopped fresh marjoram or 1 teaspoon dried marjoram

12 black olives

250 g (8 oz) mozarella or Edam cheese, sliced thinly

Oven temperature:
Gas Mark 6/200°C/400°F

This pizza has a moist and tasty filling. It can be made in advance and reheated in a hot oven for 10 minutes when needed. It can also be eaten cold.

Preheat the oven. Put the flour into a bowl with the salt and bicarbonate of soda. Make a well in the centre and put in the oil and yogurt. Mix these ingredients together to form a dough. Turn the dough on to a floured work surface and knead it lightly until it is smooth.

Roll the dough into a 27 cm (11-inch) round. Put it into a 25 cm (10-inch) greased pizza tin or pizza plate. Fold over the edges. Prick the base all over with a fork.

Scald, skin and finely chop 350 g (12 oz) of the tomatoes. Heat the oil in a frying pan on a low heat. Put in the onion, garlic and peppers and cook them until the onion is soft. Put in the chopped tomatoes and herbs. Simmer, uncovered, for 10 minutes. Take the pan from the heat. Stone and quarter 8 of the olives. Mix them into the tomato mixture.

Pour the tomato mixture on top of the pizza base and lay the cheese on top. Quarter the remaining olives and slice the remaining tomatoes. Arrange them on the top of the pizza. Bake the pizza for 25 minutes or until the edges colour.

Note: for a pizza for 2 servings, use half quantities and make the base 18 cm (7 inches) in diameter. It is not really practical to make one small enough for one serving; make enough for 2 and reheat it on another day, or eat it cold.

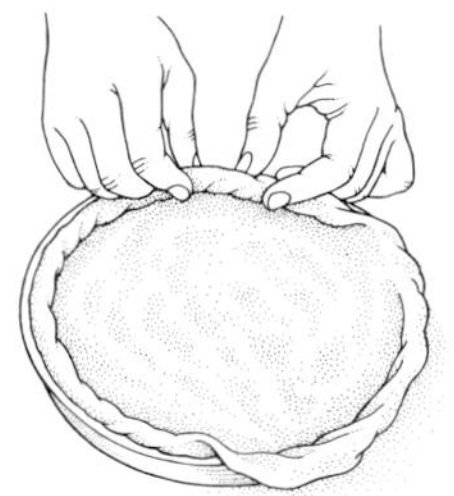

SESAME-TOPPED AUBERGINES

Preparation time: 35 minutes + 10 minutes cooking | Serves 4

2 small aubergines

2 teaspoons fine sea salt

2 tablespoons tahini (sesame paste)

2 tablespoons tomato purée

juice of 1 lemon

1 clove of garlic, crushed

1 teaspoon paprika

¼ teaspoon Tabasco sauce

2 tablespoons sesame oil or sunflower oil

4 tablespoons sesame seeds

Grilled aubergine halves have a deliciously melting texture, combined here with a tangy dressing and a crispy topping.

Cut the aubergines in half lengthways, score the cut surfaces twice and sprinkle them with the salt. Leave them, cut side down, in a colander for 30 minutes to drain.

Put the tahini into a bowl and work in the tomato purée, lemon juice, garlic, paprika and Tabasco sauce so you have a smooth paste.

Heat the grill to high. Rinse the aubergines under cold water and dry them with kitchen paper towelling. Brush them with oil. Lay them on the grill rack, cut side down and grill them for 2–3 minutes, so they begin to feel soft. Turn them over and cook them for a further 2 minutes. Spread the cut sides of the aubergine halves with the tahini paste and sprinkle the sesame seeds over the top. Return the aubergines to the grill for 1 minute for the sesame seeds to brown.

Sesame-topped Aubergines
Sardine Pasties

SARDINE PASTIES

Basic recipe: Shortcrust Pastry (page 87) Serves 4

Preparation time: 20 minutes + 45 minutes baking

- *2 × 124 g (4 oz) can of sardines in oil*
- *2 tablespoons tomato purée*
- *150 g (5 oz) potatoes, peeled and chopped finely*
- *4 small tomatoes, skinned and chopped*
- *1 small onion, chopped finely*
- *½ teaspoon paprika*
- *3 tablespoons chopped fresh parsley*
- *shortcrust pastry made with 250 g (8 oz) wholemeal flour*
- *1 egg, beaten*

Oven temperature:
Gas Mark 4/180°C/350°F

These pasties are good for picnics and packed lunches and they can also be eaten hot.

Mash the sardines with their oil and the tomato purée. Mix the sardines, potatoes, tomatoes and onion together and add the paprika and parsley.

Preheat the oven. Divide the pastry into four. Roll each piece into a round and put one quarter of the sardine mixture on one side. Fold the other side over and seal the edges. Lay the pasties on a floured baking sheet and brush them with the beaten egg.

Bake the pasties for 45 minutes. If they look as if they are going to brown too quickly, cover them with damp greaseproof paper after the first 25 minutes.

A HOT DISH OF MUSHROOMS AND ANCHOVIES

Preparation time: 35 minutes Serves 4

350 g (12 oz) open mushrooms
20 green olives
8 flat anchovy fillets
250 g (8 oz) tomatoes
4 tablespoons olive oil
1 large onion, quartered and sliced thinly
1 clove of garlic, crushed
1 teaspoon dried basil
2 tablespoons tomato purée
2 tablespoons white wine vinegar

The basil and vinegar dressing on these mushrooms gives a fresh, slightly sharp flavour, making a first course to wake up your appetite!

Thinly slice the mushrooms. Stone and quarter the olives. Finely chop the anchovies. Scald, skin and chop the tomatoes.

Heat the oil in a saucepan on a low heat. Mix in the onion and garlic. Cover, and cook gently for 10 minutes. Add the mushrooms and basil, cover again and cook for 10 minutes more. Mix in the tomato purée and vinegar, olives, anchovies and tomatoes. Simmer, uncovered, for 1 minute.

Serve in small bowls accompanied by warm wholemeal rolls.

MUSHROOM TOASTS

Preparation time: 20 minutes Serves 4

15 g (½ oz) butter or vegetable margarine
1 medium-size onion, sliced thinly
12 oz (350 g) open mushrooms, sliced thinly
2 tablespoons chopped fresh thyme
4 tablespoons chopped fresh parsley
250 g (8 oz) curd cheese
4 teaspoons Dijon mustard
8 large slices of wholemeal bread, toasted

Mushrooms on toast are always a favourite. The curd cheese used here gives them a low-calorie but creamy-textured sauce.

Melt the butter or margarine in a frying pan on a low heat. Put in the onion and soften it. Raise the heat to medium. Put in the mushrooms and herbs. Stir them for 2 minutes. Take the pan from the heat. Mix in the cheese and the Dijon mustard.

Spread the toast with butter or margarine if you want and pile the mushroom mixture on top.

LAMB IN THE POT WITH BEANS

Basic recipe: Chicken Stock (page 9) Serves 4

Preparation time: 20 minutes + 2 hours soaking + 2 hours cooking

250 g (8 oz) cannellini beans

500 g (1 lb) lean, boneless lamb

4 large sticks of celery, chopped

1 large onion, sliced thinly

1 tablespoon chopped fresh thyme or 1 teaspoon dried thyme

2 teaspoons chopped fresh rosemary or 1 teaspoon dried rosemary

600 ml (1 pint) chicken stock

300 ml (½ pint) tomato juice

½ teaspoon Tabasco sauce

2 teaspoons paprika

1 clove of garlic, crushed

Oven temperature:
Gas Mark 4/180°C/350°F

This is a simpler version of a French Cassoulet, in which haricot beans and lamb are cooked together with vegetables and seasonings. The beans enrich and thicken the dish whilst picking up the flavours of the lamb and other ingredients. A simple leafy salad would be a good accompaniment.

Put the beans into a saucepan. Cover them with water, bring them to the boil and cook them for 10 minutes. Take them from the heat and leave them to soak for 2 hours. Drain them.

Preheat the oven. Cut the lamb into 2 cm (¾-inch) dice. Layer the beans, lamb, celery, onion and herbs in a deep casserole. Mix the rest of the ingredients together and pour them over the lamb and beans. Cover the casserole and cook it in the oven for 2 hours, or until the beans and lamb are really tender.

Lamb in the Pot with Beans

WHEATY BEEF BURGERS

Basic recipe: Chicken Stock (page 9) — Serves 4

Preparation time: 30 minutes + 30 minutes chilling + 15 minutes cooking

125 g (4 oz) fresh wholemeal breadcrumbs
6 tablespoons chicken stock
2 tablespoons soy sauce
500 g (1 lb) minced beef
2 tablespoons wheatgerm
1 small onion, grated finely
1 teaspoon dried thyme
½ teaspoon dried sage
2 tablespoons tomato purée

Wholemeal breadcrumbs add fibre and give a lovely texture to minced beef in these easily-made burgers which will please all the family.

Soak the breadcrumbs in the stock and soy sauce for 15 minutes. Put the beef into a mixing bowl. Add the soaked crumbs and then all the remaining ingredients. Mix well, squeezing the mixture together with your fingers.

Form the mixture into 8 round, flat burger shapes. Lay them on a board or flat plate and refrigerate them for 30 minutes to allow them to hold their shape.

When you are ready to cook the burgers, heat the grill to high, and, if you have an open wire grill rack, cover it with foil. Lay the burgers on the hot rack and grill them for about 7 minutes on each side, or until they are browned on the outside and cooked through.

BROWN LENTIL MACARONI

Basic recipe: Vegetable Stock (page 9) Serves 4

Preparation time: 1 hour 20 minutes

250 g (8 oz) aubergines

2 teaspoons fine sea salt

2 green peppers, de-seeded

1 red pepper, de-seeded

4 tablespoons sunflower oil

1 large onion, sliced thinly

1 clove of garlic, chopped finely

250 g (8 oz) brown lentils

1 teaspoon paprika

¼ teaspoon chilli powder

300 ml (½ pint) vegetable stock

300 ml (½ pint) tomato and vegetable juice

1 bay leaf

250 g (8 oz) wholewheat macaroni

25 g (1 oz) butter or vegetable margarine

3 tablespoons wholemeal flour

300 ml (½ pint) milk

125 g (4 oz) Red Leicester cheese, grated

If the small, brown lentils are not available for this dish, use the larger green lentils instead, but do not use split red lentils as they will soften too much. The Red Leicester cheese gives a smooth and attractive flavour to this nutritious and tasty dish.

Dice the aubergines, Put them into a colander, sprinkle them with the salt, and leave them to drain for 15 minutes. Rinse them under cold water. Dry them with kitchen paper towelling.

Cut the peppers into 2.5 cm (1-inch) strips. Heat the oil in a saucepan on a low heat. Put in the onion and garlic and soften them. Add the peppers and aubergine. Cover the pan and cook for 5 minutes. Stir in the lentils, paprika and chilli powder and cook them for 1 minute. Pour in the stock and tomato and vegetable juice, add the bay leaf and bring the mixture to the boil. Re-cover the pan and cook gently for 50 minutes or until the lentils are soft.

Cook the macaroni in lightly salted boiling water for about 12 minutes or until it is just cooked through. Drain it, run cold water through it and drain it again.

To make the sauce, melt the butter or margarine on a medium heat. Stir in the flour and then the milk, gradually. Bring the sauce to the boil, stirring. Simmer for 2 minutes or until the sauce is thick. Take the pan from the heat and beat in three-quarters of the cheese.

To serve, remove the bay leaf and layer the lentil mixture and the marcaroni in a flameproof 20 cm (8-inch) serving dish or individual dishes, ending with macaroni. Pour the sauce over the top and then sprinkle on the remaining cheese. Put the dish under a hot grill for a couple of minutes.

GRILLED MACKEREL WITH MINT AND PARSLEY

Preparation time: 20 minutes + 12 minutes cooking — Serves 4

4 small or medium-size mackerel

4 tablespoons olive oil

juice of 1 lemon

4 tablespoons chopped fresh mint or 1½ teaspoons dried mint

6 tablespoons chopped fresh parsley

freshly ground black pepper

A herb and lemon baste will keep whole mackerel moist while they cook under the grill.

Clean the mackerel and cut their tails into neat V-shapes as shown in the diagram on page 39. The heads can be cut off or left, according to preference. Make three diagonal slits on each side of the mackerel, running backwards and downwards from head to tail.

Beat together the oil, lemon juice and pepper and brush the mackerel with the mixture, making sure it goes inside the slits. Mix the herbs together and stuff them into the slits in the mackerel. Heat the grill to high and, if you have an open wire rack, cover it with foil. Lay the mackerel on the hot rack and baste them with any remaining oil and lemon. Grill them for about 6 minutes on each side so they are cooked through and beginning to brown.

Grilled Mackerel with Mint and Parsley

Brown Lentil Macaroni

Herby Beef and Mushrooms

HERBY BEEF AND MUSHROOMS

Basic recipe: Chicken Stock (page 9) Serves 4

Preparation time: 25 minutes + 1¼ hours cooking

750 g (1½ lb) lean braising steak

600 ml (1 pint) chicken stock

1 large onion, sliced thinly

250 g (8 oz) open mushrooms, sliced thinly

1 tablespoon chopped fresh thyme or 1 teaspoon dried thyme

1 tablespoon chopped fresh marjoram or 1 teaspoon dried marjoram

1 tablespoon chopped fresh savory or 1 teaspoon dried savory

4 fresh sage leaves, chopped, or ½ teaspoon dried sage

Oven temperature:
Gas Mark 4/180°C/350°F

By rapidly boiling the onion in a small amount of stock and then searing the meat in the same pan, you can obtain a richly-flavoured, braised dish without the use of fat.

Preheat the oven. Cut the beef into 2 cm × 4 cm (¾-inch × 1½-inch) pieces.

Put 150 ml (¼ pint) stock into a flameproof casserole. Bring it to the boil. Put in the onion and boil it rapidly, uncovered, until the stock has reduced to about 2 tablespoons. Put in the pieces of beef and stir them on the heat until they have browned all over. Pour in the remaining stock and bring it to the boil. Put in the mushrooms and herbs. Cover the casserole and put it into the oven for 1¼ hours or until the beef is tender.

Note: for 1 or 2 servings, still use 150 ml (¼ pint) stock for cooking the onion. Then add 300 ml (½ pint) stock for 350 g (12 oz) beef; 225 ml (8 fl oz) stock for 175 g (6 oz) beef.

TROUT BAKED WITH BACON AND APPLES

Preparation time: 10 minutes + 25 minutes cooking Serves 4

4 trout weighing about 250 g (8 oz) each

1 tablespoon chopped fresh thyme or 1 teaspoon dried thyme

1 tablespoon chopped fresh marjoram or 1 teaspoon dried marjoram

2 tablespoons chopped fresh parsley

2 medium-size Bramley apples, peeled, cored and quartered

4 long rashers of lean back bacon

6 tablespoons dry cider

Oven temperature:
Gas Mark 6/200°C/400°F

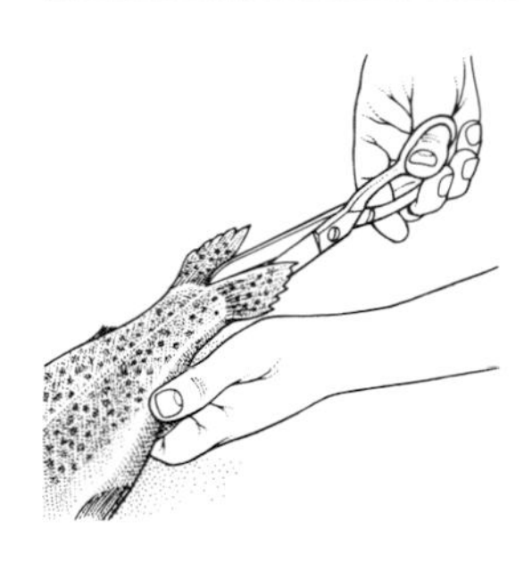

Apples complement both oily fish and pork, so a small portion of softened apple cubes goes well with this smoky-flavoured dish.

Preheat the oven. Clean the trout and cut the tails into neat V-shapes as shown in the diagram. Cut off the heads. Mix the herbs together and scatter them inside the trout.

From one of the apple quarters, cut four thin, lengthways slices and put a slice inside each fish. Wrap a bacon rasher round each fish. Lay the fish in a large, flat, ovenproof dish.

Cut the remaining apples into 1 cm (½-inch) cubes and scatter them round the trout. Pour in the cider.

Bake the trout, uncovered, for 25 minutes. If possible, serve them straight from the dish, putting one trout and a portion of apple cubes on to each plate.

Note: for 1 or 2 servings, use all the 6 table-spoons of cider.

PLAICE STEAMED WITH RED PEPPERS

Preparation time: 20 minutes + 15 minutes cooking — Serves 4

8 plaice fillets weighing about 125 g (4 oz) each

2 red peppers, de-seeded

juice of 1 lemon

2 tablespoons soy sauce

1 teaspoon ground ginger

oil for greasing

For the sauce:

4 tablespoons soy sauce

2 teaspoons tomato purée

4 tablespoons sunflower oil

Cooking fish in foil keeps in all the natural juices. Peppers and soy sauce give it a hint of a Chinese flavour.

Cut the plaice fillets in half lengthways. Cut each pepper into 8 pieces. Mix together the lemon juice and soy sauce. Brush this over the pieces of plaice and reserve the rest. Sprinkle the plaice with the ground ginger. Put a piece of pepper on the tail end of each plaice and roll the pieces up.

Put 2 plaice rolls on each of eight 25 cm (10-inch) pieces of oiled foil. Bring the edges of the foil together, fold them over and seal them. Put them into a steamer. Bring a large pan of water to the boil, lower the steamer in, and steam the plaice for 15 minutes.

Meanwhile, mix the remaining soy sauce and lemon juice with the sauce ingredients. Put them into a saucepan and bring the sauce to simmering point, but do not let it boil.

Unwrap each parcel of fish and place the rolls on warmed dinner plates. Serve the sauce separately.

Note: if no large steamer is available, use a heatproof colander, covered with foil; balance it over a large pan of lightly boiling water.

HADDOCK AND TOMATO PARCELS

Preparation time: 10 minutes + 30 minutes marinating + 20 minutes cooking

Serves 4

1 kg (2 lb) fresh haddock fillets, skinned

juice of 1 lemon

25 g (1 oz) butter or vegetable margarine

2 tablespoons fresh chopped basil or 2 teaspoons dried basil

4 large tomatoes

freshly ground black pepper

Oven temperature:
Gas Mark 4/180°C/350°F

This is another way of cooking fish in foil, this time in the oven. The tomatoes and basil give a light, fresh flavour.

Cut the fish into strips about 1 cm (½-inch) wide. Put them on a plate, sprinkle them with the lemon juice and leave them for at least 30 minutes at room temperature.

Preheat the oven. Use the butter or margarine to grease four pieces of foil each about 30 cm (12-inches) square. Put a portion of fish in the centre of each piece of foil. Sprinkle the fish with the pepper and basil. Scald, skin, de-seed and slice the tomatoes and put the slices on top of the fish. Seal the edges of the foil securely and put the parcels of fish on a baking sheet. Put them into the oven for 20 minutes.

To serve, unwrap each parcel of fish on to a separate, warmed dinner plate.

CHICKEN, AVOCADO AND SUNFLOWER SALAD

Preparation time: 45 minutes + 50 minutes cooking + cooling   Serves 4

1.2 kg (2½ lb) roasting chicken

2 teaspoons curry powder

1 carrot, split lengthways

1 stick of celery, chopped roughly

1 onion, halved

a bouquet garni sachet

1 bay leaf

1 teaspoon black peppercorns

2 oz (50 g) dried apricots

150 ml (¼ pint) orange juice

2 ripe avocados

50 g (2 oz) sunflower seeds

For the dressing:

90 ml (3 fl oz) natural yogurt

¼ teaspoon curry powder

1 clove of garlic, crushed

Poaching a chicken with herbs, vegetables and spices will give it a moist texture and delicate flavour. Add avocados and sunflower seeds to make a light salad for a main course. The excellent stock which is produced when the chicken is cooked could be used in any of the soup recipes in this book. *(See pages 9–19.)*

Rub the chicken with the curry powder. Put it into a saucepan with the carrot, celery, onion, bouquet garni, bay leaf and peppercorns. Pour in water just to cover the legs. Bring it to the boil, cover, and simmer for 50 minutes or until the chicken is tender. Lift out the chicken and cool it completely for at least 4 hours or overnight.

Soak the apricots in the orange juice for at least 4 hours.

Cut all the chicken meat from the bones and dice it. Peel, stone and dice one and a half avocados. Cut the remaining half-avocado into thin strips. Drain and finely chop the apricots.

In a bowl, mix the chicken, diced avocado, apricots and sunflower seeds. Beat together the yogurt, curry powder and garlic. Fold the resulting dressing into the salad. Put the salad on to a serving plate and garnish it with the reserved strips of avocado. Serve immediately.

Note: to make a meal for 1 person, use a small chicken portion or a poussin and quarter the other ingredients. Chicken portions or a very small roasting chicken can be used for 2 people.

GREEN PEPPER AND COTTAGE CHEESE SOUFFLÉ

Preparation time: 10 minutes + 35 minutes cooking — Serves 4

15 g (½ oz) butter, plus extra for greasing

25 g (1 oz) dry wholemeal breadcrumbs

1 large onion, sliced thinly

1 clove of garlic, chopped finely

2 medium-size green peppers, de-seeded and chopped finely

6 green olives, stoned and chopped

6 anchovy fillets, chopped

2 teaspoons chopped fresh thyme or 1 teaspoon dried thyme

4 tablespoons chopped fresh parsley

250 g (8 oz) cottage cheese

4 eggs, separated

Oven temperature:
Gas Mark 5/190°C/375°F

This soufflé is light, low in calories and easy to make. The anchovies give a lift to the flavour, but can be omitted for a completely vegetarian dish.

Butter a 900 ml (1½-pint) soufflé dish and coat the inside with crumbs. Butter a sheet of greaseproof paper that is twice as high as the dish and coat half of it with crumbs too. Tie it round the dish. Preheat the oven.

Melt the remaining butter in a frying pan on a low heat. Put in the onion and garlic and cook them until they are just beginning to turn golden. Add the peppers, cover the pan and cook for a further 10 minutes. Take the pan from the heat and let the contents cool.

Mix the olives, anchovies and herbs into the cheese. Beat in the egg yolks. Mix in the peppers and onions. Stiffly whip the egg whites. Fold them into the cheese mixture and quickly pile the mixture into the prepared soufflé dish. Bake the soufflé for 35 minutes and serve immediately.

PORK CHOPS WITH MUSTARD SEEDS

Preparation time: 10 minutes + 45 minutes cooking — Serves 4

4 tablespoons mustard powder

2 teaspoons mustard seeds

6 fresh sage leaves, chopped, or 1 teaspoon dried sage

2 teaspoons chopped fresh rosemary or 1 teaspoon dried rosemary

125 ml (4 fl oz) dry cider

4 pork chops

Oven temperature:
Gas Mark 6/200°C/400°F

Preheat the oven. Mix together the mustard powder and seeds, herbs and cider and spread the mixture over both sides of the chops.

Put the chops on a foil-lined rack in a roasting tin and cook them in the oven for 45 minutes or until they are browned and cooked through.

Pork Chops with Mustard Seeds

Tuna and Haricot Bean Salad

Broccoli and Walnut Lasagne

BROCCOLI AND WALNUT LASAGNE

Preparation time: 1 hour + 15 minutes cooking — Serves 4

750 g (1½ lb) calabrese or sprouting broccoli

500 g (1 lb) tomatoes

3 tablespoons olive oil

1 large onion, sliced thinly

1 clove of garlic, chopped finely

125 g (4 oz) walnuts, chopped finely

250 g (8 oz) wholewheat lasagne

175 g (6 oz) Cheddar cheese, grated

25 g (1 oz) butter or vegetable margarine

2 tablespoons wholemeal flour

1 teaspoon mustard powder

300 ml (½ pint) milk

Oven temperature:
Gas Mark 6/200°C/400°F

Broccoli, walnuts and tomatoes make an unusual and tasty filling to a cheese-topped lasagne that is a complete meal in itself.

Cut the broccoli into small pieces. Scald, skin and chop the tomatoes.

Heat the oil in a saucepan on a low heat. Put in the onion and garlic and soften them. Put in the broccoli and tomatoes. Cover the pan and cook on a medium heat for 15 minutes or until the broccoli is just tender. Take the pan from the heat and mix in the walnuts.

Preheat the oven. Cook the lasagne in lightly salted boiling water for 12 minutes or until it is just tender. Drain it. Rinse it with cold water and drain it again.

Put one third of the lasagne in the bottom of a 25 cm (10-inch) square, 5 cm (2-inch) deep, ovenproof dish. Put in one third of the broccoli and walnut mixture and 25 g (1 oz) of the cheese. Repeat these layers twice, the last time adding no cheese.

Melt the butter or margarine in a saucepan on a medium heat. Stir in the flour, mustard powder and milk. Bring to the boil, stirring, and simmer for 2 minutes to make a thick sauce. Take the pan from the heat and beat in about two thirds of the remaining cheese. Pour the sauce over the lasagne. Scatter the remaining cheese over the top. Put the dish into the oven for 15 minutes for the cheese to melt and begin to brown.

TUNA AND HARICOT BEAN SALAD

Preparation time: 30 minutes + 2 hours soaking + 1½ hours cooking

Serves 4

250 g (8 oz) haricot beans

200 g (7 oz) can of tuna fish, drained and flaked

1 red pepper, de-seeded

350 g (12 oz) tomatoes

250 g (8 oz) chicory, sliced thinly

4 tablespoons chopped fresh parsley

4 tablespoons mayonnaise

2 tablespoons natural yogurt

juice of 1 lemon

1 clove of garlic, crushed

freshly ground black pepper

Put the beans in a saucepan and cover them with water. Bring them to the boil and cook them rapidly for 10 minutes. Take them from the heat and leave them to soak for 2 hours. In fresh water, bring them to the boil again, boil for 10 minutes and then simmer them, covered, for 1½ hours or until they are soft. Drain them and leave them to cool.

Mix the tuna fish with the haricot beans. Cut the pepper into 2.5 cm (1-inch) long strips about 5 mm (¼-inch) wide. Chop three quarters of the tomatoes and mix these, the chicory, pepper and half the parsley into the tuna and beans.

Mix together the mayonnaise, yogurt, lemon juice, garlic and pepper. Fold this dressing into thc salad.

Arrange the salad on a serving plate. Garnish it with the remaining tomatoes, cut into wedges or slices, and scatter the remaining parsley over the top.

SWEET AND SOUR PEANUTS

Preparation time: 30 minutes | Serves 4

- *half a small pineapple*
- *1 green pepper, de-seeded and halved*
- *1 tablespoon cornflour*
- *2 teaspoons soy sauce*
- *5 tablespoons cider vinegar*
- *1 tablespoon clear honey*
- *3 tablespoons sunflower oil*
- *1 large onion, sliced thinly*
- *1 clove of garlic, chopped finely*
- *125 g (4 oz) unsalted peanuts, shelled*
- *225 g (8 oz) can of bamboo shoots, drained and sliced thinly*
- *230 g (8 oz) can of water chestnuts, drained and sliced thinly*

This is a dish with a definite Chinese character. Assemble all the ingredients before you start to cook and you will find it easy and very quick to make. Serve this with plain rice.

Cut the skin from the pineapple. Cut the flesh into slices, stamp out the cores with an apple corer or cut them out with a knife. Cut the flesh into 2 cm (¾-inch) dice. Cut the pepper into 2 cm (¾-inch) squares. Put the cornflour into a bowl and gradually mix in the soy sauce, vinegar and honey.

Heat the oil in a wok or large frying pan on a low heat. Put in the pepper, onion and garlic and stir-fry them for 2 minutes. Put in the peanuts, bamboo shoots and water chestnuts and stir-fry for 2 minutes more. Mix in the pineapple.

Stir the cornflour mixture. Pour it into the pan. Simmer, stirring, until the mixture thickens to a small amount of glossy sauce. Take the pan from the heat and serve as soon as possible.

Egg and Almond Stir-fry
Sweet and Sour Peanuts

EGG AND ALMOND STIR-FRY

Preparation time: 40 minutes | Serves 4

250 g (8 oz) long grain brown rice

4 tablespoons sunflower oil

1 small or medium-size green cabbage, shredded

1 clove of garlic, chopped finely

125 g (4 oz) almonds, shelled

1 teaspoon hot Madras curry powder

1 teaspoon ground turmeric

6 hard-boiled eggs, chopped

Quickly stir-fried cabbage and almonds make a crisp contrast to chopped hard-boiled eggs and curry-flavoured rice.

Cook the rice in lightly salted water for 40 minutes or until it is just tender. Drain it, run cold water through it and drain it again.

Heat the oil in a wok or a very large frying pan on a high heat. Put in the cabbage and garlic and stir-fry them for about 3 minutes or until the cabbage begins to soften. Mix in the almonds, rice, curry powder and turmeric and stir for a further 2 minutes. Mix in the eggs and stir for about half a minute to heat them through. Serve as soon as possible.

Note: this is a one-dish meal for which no accompaniment is necessary.

EGG-TOPPED CHEESY COURGETTES

Preparation time: 20 minutes | Serves 4

25 g (2 oz) butter or vegetable margarine

1 kg (2 lb) small courgettes, grated coarsely

4 tablespoons chopped fresh parsley

1 clove of garlic, chopped finely

250 g (8 oz) tomatoes, chopped

125 g (4 oz) Cheddar cheese, grated finely

8 eggs

Grated courgettes and Cheddar cheese make an unusual 'bed' for lightly poached eggs.

Melt the butter in a saucepan on a high heat. Put in the courgettes, parsley and garlic and stir for 3 minutes, or until the courgettes are just beginning to soften. Mix in the tomatoes and stir for 1 minute to heat them through. Take the pan from the heat and mix in the cheese.

Pour the courgette mixture into a flat serving dish and keep it warm. Poach the eggs and place them on top. Serve at once.

SPICED PINTO BEANS WITH SAVOURY RICE

Basic recipe: Vegetable Stock (page 9) Serves 4

Preparation time: 15 minutes + 2 hours soaking + 2 hours cooking

For the beans:

250 g (8 oz) pinto beans

750 ml (1¼ pints) vegetable stock

2 large onions, chopped finely

1 garlic clove, chopped finely

2 tablespoons chopped fresh savory

2 bay leaves

4 allspice berries, crushed, or a pinch of ground allspice

6 black peppercorns, crushed

1 tablespoon tomato purée

150 g (5.29 oz) carton of natural yogurt

juice of 1 lemon

For the savoury rice:

2 tablespoons oil

1 medium-size onion, sliced thinly

250 g (8 oz) long grain brown rice

600 ml (1 pint) vegetable stock

1 tablespoon tomato purée

1 bay leaf

To garnish:

3 tablespoons chopped fresh parsley (optional)

Oven temperature:
Gas Mark 2/150°C/300°F

Spicy beans and rice make an all-in-one meal. This is best served with salad.

Put the beans into a saucepan and cover them with water. Bring them to the boil, and cook rapidly for 10 minutes. Take them from the heat and leave them to soak for 2 hours. Drain them.

Preheat the oven. Put 150 ml (¼ pint) stock into a flameproof casserole and bring it to the boil. Put in the onions and garlic. Cook them rapidly, uncovered, until the stock is reduced to 2 tablespoons. Pour in the remaining stock and bring it to the boil. Add the beans, savory, bay leaves, allspice, peppercorns and tomato purée. Cover the casserole and put it into the oven for 2 hours or until the beans are quite soft.

Prepare the rice while the beans are cooking. Heat the oil in a saucepan on a low heat. Put in the onion and soften it. Stir in the rice and cook it for 1 minute. Pour in the stock and bring it to the boil. Add the tomato purée and bay leaf. Cover the pan and simmer for 40 minutes or until the rice is soft and all the liquid has been absorbed.

Take the casserole from the oven and let the beans come off the boil. Stir in the yogurt and lemon juice. To serve, spoon the rice into a shallow serving dish, and pour the beans on top. Garnish with the chopped parsley if you like.

Note: for 2 persons, use 450 ml (¾ pint) stock to cook the rice; for 1 person, 300 ml (½ pint) stock. Halve or quarter the rest of the ingredients accordingly.

VEGETABLE SHEPHERD'S PIE

Basic recipe: Vegetable Stock (page 9) Serves 4

Preparation time: 1 hour + 20 minutes cooking

125 g (4 oz) split red lentils

50 g (2 oz) pot barley or pearl barley

250 g (8 oz) carrots, grated

1 medium-size onion, chopped finely

397 g (14 oz) can of tomatoes

300 ml (½ pint) vegetable stock

750 g (1½ lb) potatoes

6 tablespoons milk

75 g (3 oz) Cheddar cheese, grated

Oven temperature:
Gas Mark 6/200°C/400°F

Red lentils, barley and vegetables make a tasty, meatless, protein-packed shepherd's pie. Pot barley is the whole barley grains, but pearl barley makes a good substitute if none is available.

Put the lentils, barley, carrots, onion, tomatoes and their juice and stock into a saucepan. Bring them to the boil, cover the pan, and simmer for 40 minutes or until the lentils and barley are soft. Boil the potatoes in their skins. Peel them as soon as they are cool enough to handle and mash them with the milk and cheese.

Preheat the oven. Put the lentil mixture into a 900 ml (1½ pint) pie dish. Pile the potatoes on top in an even layer. Make patterns on them with a fork. Put the pie into the oven for 20 minutes or until the ridges on top begin to brown.

Note: a low-fat Cheddar-type cheese may be used instead of the full-fat variety.

NUTTY STUFFED AUBERGINES

Basic recipe: Vegetable Stock (page 9) Serves 4

Preparation time: 30 minutes + 15 minutes cooking

2 aubergines, weighing about 350 g (12 oz) each

3 tablespoons oil, plus extra for greasing

1 medium-size onion, chopped finely

1 clove of garlic, chopped finely

150 g (5 oz) fresh wholemeal breadcrumbs

75 g (3 oz) hazelnuts, ground

75 g (3 oz) cashew nuts, ground

1 tablespoon tomato purée

125 ml (4 fl oz) vegetable stock

1 tablespoon chopped fresh thyme or 1 teaspoon dried thyme

1 tablespoon chopped fresh marjoram or 1 teaspoon dried marjoram

Oven temperature:
Gas Mark 6/200°C/400°F

Baked aubergines make delicious soft containers for a tomato-flavoured nut roast mixture.

Preheat the oven. Trim the stalks from the aubergines. Wrap each aubergine separately in oiled foil and put them into the oven for 15–20 minutes. Cut the aubergines in half lengthways and scoop out the centres, leaving shells about 1 cm (½-inch) thick. Chop and reserve half the scooped-out flesh.

Heat the oil in a frying pan on a low heat. Put in the onion and garlic and cook them until they are soft and golden. Take the pan from the heat. Mix in all the remaining ingredients plus the chopped aubergine.

Pile the mixture back into the aubergine shells. Place the aubergines in an oiled, ovenproof dish and bake them for 15 minutes.

GINGERED CHICKEN WITH TOMATO YOGURT

Preparation time: 15 minutes + 45 minutes cooking | Serves 4

1.5 kg (3½ lb) roasting chicken

150 g (5.29 oz) carton of natural yogurt

juice of ½ a lemon

2 tablespoons tomato purée

50 g (2 oz) root ginger

1 clove of garlic, crushed

Oven temperature:
Gas Mark 6/200°C/400°F

These chicken pieces have a red-brown crispy skin and the light, gently spicy flavour of fresh ginger. If no fresh ginger is available, use 1 teaspoon ground ginger.

Preheat the oven. Joint the chicken and lay the joints, skin side up, in an ovenproof dish.

Mix together the yogurt, lemon juice and tomato purée. Peel the ginger and grate it directly into the yogurt mixture. Mix in the garlic. Spoon the mixture over the chicken pieces.

Put the chicken into the oven and cook for 45 minutes or until the skin crisps and browns. Serve straight from the dish.

Note: for 1 or 2 servings, use chicken portions.

BROWN RICE SALAD WITH CHEESE

Preparation time: 40 minutes + 30 minutes standing — Serves 4

- *250 g (8 oz) long grain brown rice*
- *a pinch of sea salt*
- *4 tablespoons olive oil*
- *2 tablespoons white wine vinegar*
- *1 clove of garlic, crushed with a pinch of sea salt*
- *2 tablespoons chopped fresh thyme or 1½ teaspoons dried thyme*
- *50 g (2 oz) Edam cheese, grated*
- *1 green pepper, de-seeded and chopped finely*
- *125 g (4 oz) button mushrooms, sliced thinly*
- *250 g (8 oz) tomatoes, chopped finely*
- *freshly ground black pepper*

Serve this salad with any cold dish. If you add a little extra cheese it can become a main meal in itself.

Put the rice into a saucepan with the salt and 600 ml (1 pint) water. Bring it to the boil. Cover the pan and simmer for 40 minutes or until the rice is tender and all the water has been absorbed. Rinse the rice with cold water, drain it well and allow it to cool.

Beat the oil, vinegar, garlic and black pepper together. Fold them into the rice. Mix in the thyme and cheese.

Mix the green pepper and mushrooms into the rice. Leave the salad for 30 minutes. Mix in the tomatoes just before serving.

PASTA WITH TOMATO CREAM SAUCE

Preparation time: 15 minutes Serves 4

250 g (8 oz) wholewheat pasta shapes or wholewheat spaghetti or tagliatelle

150 ml (¼ pint) creamed smatana, or soured cream

juice of ½ a lemon

2 tablespoons tomato purée

1 tablespoon fresh chopped basil or 1½ teaspoons dried basil

3 tablespoons chopped fresh parsley

Serve this tomato-flavoured pasta as an accompaniment to any meat, fish or vegetarian main dish.

Cook the pasta in lightly salted boiling water for 12 minutes or until it is just tender. Drain it, run cold water through it and drain it again.

Mix together the remaining ingredients in a saucepan. Bring them to simmering point but do not let them boil. Gently fold in the pasta and let it become coated with the sauce.

Pasta with Tomato Cream Sauce
Pasta with Olives, Spring Onions and Walnuts

Brown Rice Salad with Cheese

PASTA WITH OLIVES, SPRING ONIONS AND WALNUTS

Preparation time: 20 minutes — Serves 4

- *250 g (8 oz) wholewheat pasta*
- *4 tablespoons olive oil*
- *6 spring onions, chopped*
- *1 clove of garlic, crushed*
- *10 green olives, halved and stoned*
- *50 g (2 oz) walnuts, ground or chopped finely*
- *2 tablespoons chopped fresh parsley*
- *1 tablespoon grated parmesan cheese*
- *freshly ground black pepper*

This goes best with light main dishes. Add more walnuts and Parmesan cheese to turn it into a main dish in itself.

Cook the pasta in lightly salted boiling water for 12 minutes or until it is tender. Drain it, run cold water through it and drain it again.

Heat the oil in a saucepan on a low heat. Put in the spring onions and garlic and cook them for 1 minute. Mix in the olives, walnuts and parsley, and then the pasta, parmesan cheese and pepper. Mix gently so that the pasta becomes coated with the rest of the ingredients. Serve at once.

SPICED BULGHUR SALAD

Preparation time: 30 minutes — Serves 4

- *250 g (8 oz) bulghur wheat*
- *25 g (1 oz) fresh parsley, chopped*
- *2 tablespoons natural yogurt*
- *2 tablespoons olive or sunflower oil*
- *juice of ½ a lemon*
- *¼ teaspoon ground ginger*
- *250 g (8 oz) tomatoes*

Bulghur wheat consists of wheat grains that have been soaked and then heated so that they crack into small pieces. It is also called bulgar or bulgur or sometimes burghul wheat. As it needs no cooking it is easy and quick to prepare.

Soak the wheat in warm water for 20 minutes. Drain it and squeeze it dry very thoroughly. Mix it with the parsley.

Mix together all the remaining ingredients except the tomatoes. Fold this dressing into the salad.

Put the salad into a bowl or serving dish and garnish it with the tomatoes, cut into wedges or slices.

SOY RICE WITH LEMON

Preparation time: 10 minutes + 40 minutes cooking — Serves 4

250 g (8 oz) long grain brown rice

a pinch of sea salt

1 lemon

4 tablespoons groundnut or sunflower oil

1 medium-size onion, sliced thinly

2 tablespoons soy sauce

This is a variation on Chinese fried rice. The lemon lightens the flavour, making it a light but nourishing dish.

Put the rice in a saucepan with 600 ml (1 pint) water and the salt. Bring it to the boil, cover the pan, and simmer it gently for 40 minutes, or until the rice is tender and all the water has been absorbed. Rinse the rice with cold water and drain it well.

Cut the rind and pith from the lemon and finely chop the flesh. Heat the oil in a saucepan on a low heat. Put in the onion and soften it. Fork in the rice and lemon flesh and add the soy sauce. Toss the rice on the heat for 2 minutes so it heats through.

Note: for 2 servings use 125 g (4 oz) rice and 300 ml (½ pint) water; for 1 serving use 50 g (2 oz) rice and 225 ml (8 fl oz) water.

VEGETABLE MIXED GRILL

Preparation time: 30 minutes + 30 minutes marinating   Serves 4

8 medium-size open mushrooms

4 tomatoes

4 small courgettes

one medium-size aubergine, weighing about 350 g (12 oz)

For the marinade:

125 ml (4 fl oz) olive or sunflower oil

juice of 1 lemon

2 tablespoons tomato purée

2 teaspoons paprika

a pinch of chilli powder

2 tablespoons chopped fresh thyme or 2 teaspoons dried thyme

Grilling vegetables is quick and economical. Brush them with oil, or leave them in a tasty marinade for a while before cooking.

Trim the stalks of the mushrooms leaving only about 5 mm (¼ inch). Halve the tomatoes crossways. Cut each courgette in half lengthways. Cut the aubergine into 8 slices of equal thickness.

Mix the ingredients for the marinade together. Turn the mushrooms, courgettes and aubergines in the marinade and leave them for 30 minutes. Just before cooking, brush the marinade over the tomatoes.

Heat the grill to high. Grill the courgettes for 2 minutes on each side, the aubergines for about 1½ minutes on each side, the mushrooms for 1½ minutes each side, and the tomatoes, cut-side-up only, for 2 minutes.

Arrange the cooked vegetables attractively on a serving plate.

Vegetable Mixed Grill

PEANUT AND SULTANA PILAFF

Basic recipe: Vegetable Stock (page 9) Serves 4

Preparation time: 20 minutes + 40 minutes cooking

3 tablespoons sunflower oil

1 medium-size onion, sliced thinly

1 clove of garlic, chopped

1 teaspoon ground coriander

1 teaspoon cumin seeds

250 g (8 oz) long grain brown rice

600 ml (1 pint) vegetable stock

a pinch of sea salt

40 g (1½ oz) unsalted peanuts, shelled

40 g (1½ oz) sultanas

This lightly spiced rice dish goes well with casseroles and curries.

Heat the oil in a saucepan on a low heat. Put in the onion and garlic and cook them for 2 minutes. Mix in the spices and continue cooking until the onion is soft. Add the rice and stir it for 1 minute. Pour in the stock, add the salt and bring it to the boil. Cover the pan, and cook on a low heat for 40 minutes, or until the rice is tender and all the stock has been absorbed.

Turn off the heat but leave the pan on the ring. Mix the peanuts and sultanas into the rice. Put on the lid and let the rice stand for a further 10 minutes.

Note: for 2 servings, use 125 g (4 oz) rice and 300 ml (½ pint) stock; for 1 serving use 50 g (2 oz) rice and 250 ml (8 fl oz) stock.

JACKET POTATOES WITH MUSTARD AND CRESS

Preparation time: 25 minutes + 1½ hours baking — Serves 4

4 large potatoes

6 tablespoons soured cream

½ teaspoon mustard powder

1 carton of mustard and cress

freshly ground black pepper

Oven temperature:
Gas Mark 6/200°C/400°F

Preheat the oven. Scrub the potatoes and prick each one on both sides with a fork. Put the potatoes on the oven rack and bake them for 1¼ hours or until the outsides are crisp and the middles are soft.

Cut each potato in half lengthways. Scoop the middles into a bowl and mash them; add the soured cream, mustard powder and mustard and cress and mix well. Add plenty of pepper. Pile the mixture back into the potato shells and make ridges on the top with a fork.

Put the filled potato shells in an ovenproof dish. Return them to the oven for 15 minutes or until the tops begin to brown.

JACKET POTATOES WITH APPLE AND ONION

Preparation time: 25 minutes + 1½ hours cooking — Serves 4

4 large potatoes

25 g (1 oz) butter or vegetable margarine

1 small cooking apple, peeled, cored and chopped finely

1 small onion, chopped finely

Oven temperature:
Gas Mark 6/200°C/400°F

Preheat the oven. Scrub the potatoes and prick them on both sides with a fork. Lay them on the oven rack and bake them for 1¼ hours or until they are soft.

Cut the potatoes in half lengthways. Scoop out the middles and mash them with the butter or margarine. Mix the apple and onion into the potato.

Put the potato shells in a heatproof dish. Pile the stuffing mixture inside them and make ridges on the tops with a fork. Return the potatoes to the oven for 15 minutes or until the tops are beginning to brown.

WHITE CABBAGE, GRAPEFRUIT AND GRAPE SALAD

Preparation time: 25 minutes | Serves 4

- *350 g (12 oz) white cabbage*
- *175 g (6 oz) white grapes*
- *1 large pink grapefruit*
- *4 tablespoons olive or sunflower oil*
- *juice of 1 lemon*
- *1 teaspoon Tabasco sauce*
- *1 teaspoon paprika*
- *1 clove of garlic, crushed*

This is an attractive, delicately coloured salad. The sweet grapes and the slightly bitter grapefruit complement one another and add freshness to the cabbage.

Finely shred the cabbage. Halve and de-seed the grapes. Cut the rind and pith from the grapefruit, cut the flesh into quarters and slice it thinly. Mix all 3 together in a serving bowl.

Beat the remaining ingredients together to make the dressing and fold it into the salad.

White Cabbage, Grapefruit and Grape Salad

Bulghur and Chick-pea Salad

Jacket Potatoes with Apple and Onion

BULGHUR AND CHICK-PEA SALAD

Preparation time: 30 minutes — Serves 4

- *250 g (8 oz) bulghur wheat*
- *432 g (15¼ oz) can of chick-peas*
- *½ a cucumber, chopped*
- *75 g (3 oz) unsalted peanuts, shelled*
- *4 tablespoons chopped fresh parsley*
- *2 tablespoons chopped fresh chives*
- *2 tablespoons natural yogurt*
- *2 tablespoons olive oil*
- *juice of ½ a lemon*
- *1 teaspoon curry powder*
- *1 clove of garlic, crushed*

Bulghur wheat is ideal for snack meals as it requires no cooking. Cans of cooked pulses are also excellent store-cupboard standbys.

Soak the bulghur wheat in warm water for 30 minutes. Drain it and squeeze it dry thoroughly. Put it in a bowl. Drain the chick-peas, and add these and the cucumber, peanuts and herbs to the wheat.

Beat together the remaining ingredients and fold them into the salad.

STEAMED GRATED ROOT VEGETABLES

Preparation time: 30 minutes — Serves 4

- *250 g (8 oz) carrots*
- *250 g (8 oz) swede*
- *250 g (8 oz) parsnips*
- *1 large leek*
- *¼ nutmeg, grated, or ¼ teaspoon ground nutmeg*

This is a delicious winter dish, with the rich flavour of root vegetables but a light texture.

Scrub and finely grate the carrots and swedes. Scrub the parsnips. Cut them in half and remove the woody cores. Finely grate the rest. Thinly slice the leek. Mix all these together in a vegetable steamer and season with the nutmeg.

Bring a large pan of water to the boil. Lower in the steamer. Cover the vegetables and steam them for 20 minutes, turning them once.

Note: if no steamer is available, use a steam-proof colander and cover it with foil.

MIXED SALAD WITH GRATED APPLE

Preparation time: 10 minutes — Serves 4

- *250 g (8 oz) carrots*
- *125 g (4 oz) cooked beetroot*
- *1 crisp dessert apple*
- *4 large sticks of celery*
- *75 g (3 oz) alfalfa sprouts or 2 cartons of mustard and cress*
- *4 tablespoons sunflower oil*
- *2 tablespoons cider vinegar*
- *1 clove of garlic, crushed*
- *freshly ground black pepper*

This salad has a very English flavour and is excellent with oily fish and with egg and cheese dishes.

Coarsely grate the carrots, beetroot and apple and finely chop the celery. Mix them in a bowl with the alfalfa sprouts or mustard and cress.

Beat together the remaining ingredients to make the dressing and fold it into the salad.

STIR-BRAISED CARROTS AND CAULIFLOWER

Basic recipe: Vegetable Stock (page 9) — Serves 4

Preparation time: 20 minutes

- *1 small cauliflower*
- *250 g (8 oz) carrots*
- *3 tablespoons sunflower oil*
- *175 ml (6 fl oz) vegetable stock or 150 ml (1/4 pint) stock and 4 tablespoons dry white wine*
- *1 tablespoon chopped thyme or 1 teaspoon dried thyme*
- *1 tablespoon chopped marjoram or 1 teaspoon dried marjoram*

This is another recipe based on Chinese methods. The flavours are more European, but the texture of the vegetables is still fresh and crisp.

Cut the cauliflower into very small florets. Thinly slice the carrots. Heat the oil in a wok or large frying pan on a high heat. Put in the cauliflower and carrots and stir-fry them for 2 minutes. Pour in the stock, or stock and wine, and bring it to the boil. Add the herbs, cover, and cook on a medium heat for 10 minutes by which time most of the liquid should have evaporated.

Note: for 2 servings, halve the amount of vegetables and for 1 serving quarter the amounts; in both cases use the full amount of liquid.

MILLET WITH PEPPERS

Basic recipe: Vegetable Stock (page 9) Serves 4

Preparation time: 30 minutes

- *4 tablespoons sunflower oil*
- *1 red pepper, de-seeded and diced*
- *1 green pepper, de-seeded and diced*
- *1 small onion, chopped finely*
- *1 clove of garlic, chopped finely*
- *250 g (8 oz) millet*
- *600 ml (1 pint) vegetable stock*
- *freshly ground black pepper*

Millet seeds are small and yellow, and when cooked have a light, fluffy texture and a delicate flavour. This is an ideal accompaniment to a spicy main course.

Heat the oil in a frying pan on a medium heat. Put in the peppers, onion and garlic and stir-fry them for 1 minute. Lower the heat. Put in the millet and stir it for 1 minute. Pour in the stock, bring it to the boil and season. Cover the pan and simmer on a low heat for 20 minutes or until the millet has a light, fluffy texture and all the stock has been absorbed.

Note: for 2 servings use 125 g (4 oz) millet and 350 ml (12 fl oz) stock; for 1 serving use 50 g (2 oz) millet and 250 ml (8 fl oz) stock.

Stir-braised Carrots and Cauliflower
Millet with Peppers

STIR-FRIED PEPPERS AND WATER CHESTNUTS

Preparation time: 10 minutes — Serves 4

- *2 green peppers*
- *1 red pepper*
- *230 g (8 oz) can of water chestnuts*
- *6 spring onions*
- *25 g (1 oz) root ginger*
- *4 tablespoons groundnut or sunflower oil*
- *1 clove of garlic, chopped finely*
- *125 g (4 oz) beansprouts*
- *4 tablespoons dry sherry or stock*
- *2 tablespoons soy sauce*

The Chinese method of quickly stir-frying vegetables preserves many valuable vitamins and keeps the vegetables crisp, tasty and brightly coloured.

Core and de-seed the peppers and cut them into 2 cm (¾-inch) squares. Drain and thinly slice the water chestnuts. Cut the spring onions into 2 cm (¾-inch) lengths. Peel and finely grate the root ginger.

Heat the oil in a wok or a large frying pan on a high heat. Put in the peppers, water chestnuts, spring onions, ginger and garlic and stir-fry for 2 minutes. Add the beansprouts and stir-fry for 1 minute more. Add the sherry or stock and soy sauce and stir-fry for a further 30 seconds.

CABBAGE AND LEEKS WITH DIJON MUSTARD

Basic recipe: Vegetable Stock (page 9) — Serves 4

Preparation time: 20 minutes

- *1 small green or Savoy cabbage*
- *500 g (1 lb) leeks*
- *15 g (½ oz) butter or vegetable margarine*
- *150 ml (¼ pint) vegetable stock, water or dry cider*
- *2 teaspoons Dijon mustard*
- *1 tablespoon chopped savory or 1 teaspoon dried savory*

Cabbage and leeks are a perfect savoury combination. Serve this with pork or with any egg or cheese dish.

Shred the cabbage. Thinly slice the leeks. Melt the butter or margarine in a saucepan on a high heat. Put in the cabbage and leeks and stir them around so they become evenly coated. Pour in the stock and bring it to the boil. Add the mustard and savory.

Cover the pan and cook on a low heat for 12–15 minutes. The cabbage should still be quite crisp. Drain if necessary and serve immediately.

CHINESE LEAVES, FENNEL AND TOMATO SALAD

Preparation time: 10 minutes   Serves 4

half a head of chinese leaves

1 small bulb of fennel

4 firm tomatoes

25 g (1 oz) currants

4 tablespoons olive or sunflower oil

2 tablespoons cider vinegar

1 tablespoon tomato purée

1 clove of garlic, crushed

freshly ground black pepper

This is a light, crisp-textured salad. The addition of tomatoes and currants makes it both colourful and tasty.

Chop the chinese leaves, fennel and tomatoes and put them into a salad bowl with the currants. Beat the remaining ingredients together to make the dressing and fold them into the salad.

CHICORY, RED PEPPER AND TOMATO SALAD

Preparation time: 10 minutes   Serves 4

2 heads of chicory

1 red pepper

4 large sticks of celery

1 large orange

4 tablespoons olive or sunflower oil

2 tablespoons white wine vinegar

1 teaspoon French mustard

1 clove of garlic, crushed

freshly ground black pepper

This is a lovely, colourful salad. The sweet red peppers go well with the slightly bitter chicory.

Trim the stalk ends of the chicory. Cut each head in half lengthways and then thinly slice it. Core and de-seed the pepper and cut it into 2.5 cm (1-inch) strips about 5 mm (¼-inch) wide. Chop the celery. Cut the rind and pith from the orange, cut the flesh into quarters lengthways and then thinly slice these.

In a salad bowl, mix together the chicory, pepper, celery and orange. Beat the remaining ingredients together to make the dressing and fold them into the salad.

BUCKWHEAT WITH CELERY AND CARROTS

Basic recipe: Vegetable Stock (page 9) Serves 4

Preparation time: 10 minutes + 20 minutes cooking

- *4 sticks of celery, chopped finely*
- *175 g (6 oz) carrots, chopped finely*
- *1 small onion, chopped finely*
- *250 g (8 oz) buckwheat*
- *1 egg, beaten*
- *600 ml (1 pint) vegetable stock*

Cooked buckwheat is sometimes called kasha. It has a rich, nutty flavour which combines well with all sorts of vegetables.

Finely chop the celery, carrots and onion. Heat a large, heavy frying pan on a moderate heat. Put in the buckwheat and stir it for half a minute. Pour in the egg and stir quickly so it sets round the buckwheat grains. Pour in the stock and bring it to the boil. Put in the celery, carrot and onion. Cover the pan and cook gently for 20 minutes or until the buckwheat is soft and all the stock has been absorbed.

Note: for 2 servings use 125 g (4 oz) buckwheat and 350 ml (12 fl oz) stock; for 1 serving, use 50 g (2 oz) buckwheat and 250 ml (8 fl oz) stock.

STRAWBERRY JELLY

Preparation time: 10 minutes + cooling + 2 hours chilling   Serves 4

370 g (13 oz) can of strawberries in fruit juice

11 g (½ oz) sachet of gelatine

6 tablespoons water

450 g (13 oz) carton of natural yogurt

4 tablespoons toasted flaked almonds

This jelly is an attractive pinky-purple colour with a light, refreshing flavour. The same recipe can be made with a can of raspberries in fruit juice.

Rub the strawberries with their juice through a sieve. Put them into a saucepan and heat them gently.

In a small pan, soak the gelatine in the water. Gently melt the gelatine and stir it into the strawberry purée. Remove the pan from the heat and cool the mixture completely.

Put the yogurt into a bowl and gradually mix in the strawberry purée. Pour the mixture into one large bowl or four small ones. Leave the jelly in a cool place for 2 hours to set.

Just before serving, scatter the toasted flaked almonds over the top.

APPLE AND GINGER MOUSSE

Preparation time: 30 minutes + 15 minutes cooking + 2 hours setting — Serves 4

- *500 g (1 lb) Bramley apples*
- *125 ml (4 fl oz) unsweetened apple juice*
- *4 cloves*
- *1 thinly pared strip of lemon rind*
- *11 g (½ oz) sachet of gelatine*
- *75 g (3 oz) raisins, chopped finely*
- *1 egg, separated*
- *8 pieces of preserved stem ginger, chopped*
- *150 ml (5 fl oz) soured cream*
- *4 tablespoons crunchy oat cereal*

This is a special occasion dessert. The apple juice, raisins and ginger provide all the sweetness necessary and the soured cream gives a lighter texture than double or whipping cream.

Peel, core and chop the apples. Put them into a saucepan with half the apple juice, the cloves and lemon rind. Cover them and set them on a low heat for 15 minutes or until they can be beaten to a purée.

Soak the gelatine in the remaining apple juice whilst the apples are cooking. Melt it gently on a low heat. Rub the apple purée through a sieve, mix in the raisins and then gently warm the apple purée again. Stir in the gelatine. Beat in the egg yolk. Stir the mixture with a wooden spoon on a low heat, without boiling, until it begins to thicken. Take the pan from the heat and mix in the ginger. Cool the mixture until it is on the point of setting.

Stiffly whip the egg white. Lightly whip the soured cream; it will not thicken like double or whipping cream, but will become more creamy in texture. Fold first the soured cream and then the egg white into the apple mixture. Pour the mixture into a serving dish. Leave the mousse in a cool place for 2 hours to set.

Just before serving, scatter the top with the oat cereal.

RICE RING WITH PEACHES

Preparation time: 20 minutes + 30 minutes cooking + 2 hours chilling

Serves 4

175 g (6 oz) long grain brown rice

600 ml (1 pint) apple juice

¼ teaspoon ground nutmeg

11 g (½ oz) sachet of gelatine

4 tablespoons warm water

450 g (15 oz) carton of natural yogurt

4 peaches

If fresh peaches are not available for this mould, use another fresh fruit in season, for example, pineapple or dessert plums, dessert pears, strawberries or raspberries. You could also use fruit canned in natural juices.

Put the rice into a saucepan with the apple juice and nutmeg. Bring it to the boil. Cover the pan and simmer for 30–40 minutes or until the rice is soft. Drain off excess juice if necessary.

In a small pan, soak the gelatine in the warm water and then melt it on a low heat and stir it into the rice. Leave the mixture to cool. Mix in the yogurt.

Put one peach into a bowl and pour boiling water over it. Leave it for 2 minutes and then drain it and peel off the skin. Stone and slice the peach.

Lay the peach slices in the bottom of an oiled 900 ml (1½-pint) ring mould. Spoon the rice mixture on top. Leave the mould in a cool place for 2 hours to set.

Just before serving, scald, skin and slice the remaining peaches. Turn out the rice mould and fill the centre with the sliced peaches.

Note: if you are making half or quarter the quantity, set the mould in individual bowls with sliced fruit in the base and do not turn them out. Decorate with more fruit when set. For 125 g (4 oz) rice, use 350 ml (12 fl oz) apple juice; for 50 g (2 oz) rice, use 250 ml (8 fl oz) apple juice.

CITRUS FRUIT SALAD

Preparation time: 10 minutes + 15 minutes chilling — Serves 4

2 pink grapefruit
4 medium-size oranges
2 tablespoons clear honey
2 bananas

Sweet bananas provide an excellent contrast to sharp citrus fruits in a fruit salad. Adding honey to the fruit and letting it stand for a while will draw out the juices and make a syrup. For a special occasion, add a little orange liqueur with the honey.

Cut the rind and pith from the grapefruit and oranges. Cut the fruit into segments and cut away the remaining pith. If the grapefruit segments are large, cut them in half. Put the fruit into a bowl. Fold in the honey and chill for 15 minutes.

Peel and slice the bananas and fold them into the rest of the fruit. Serve immediately.

Pineapple and Dried Fruit Salad

Rice Ring with Peaches
Citrus Fruit Salad

PINEAPPLE AND DRIED FRUIT SALAD

Preparation time: 5 minutes + 9 hours chilling Serves 4

125 g (4 oz) dried whole apricots

8 prunes

25 g (1 oz) dried apple rings

300 ml (1/2 pint) orange or pineapple juice

1 small pineapple

2 tablespoons chopped toasted hazelnuts

Sweet dried fruits and the liquid in which they have been soaking will provide all the sweetness needed for a fresh pineapple. Natural yogurt, soured cream or creamed smatana could be served with the salad as a topping.

Soak the apricots, prunes and apple rings in the orange or pineapple juice for 8 hours.

Cut the skin from the pineapple. Slice it, remove the cores and chop the slices. Mix the pineapple with the dried fruits and juice and chill for a further hour. Add more fruit juice if you wish.

Put the fruit salad into serving bowls, scatter the toasted hazelnuts over the top and serve at once.

STEAMED CAROB PUDDING WITH PINEAPPLE SAUCE

Preparation time: 15 minutes + 1½ hours cooking Serves 4

For the pudding:

75 g (3 oz) stoned dates, chopped finely

90 ml (3 fl oz) unsweetened pineapple juice

125 g (4 oz) wholemeal flour

1 teaspoon bicarbonate of soda

50 g (2 oz) carob powder, sieved

125 g (4 oz) butter or vegetable margarine, plus extra for greasing

2 eggs, beaten

For the sauce:

1 tablespoon arrowroot

300 ml (½ pint) unsweetened pineapple juice

This is a hearty family dessert. The pudding is light and sweet although completely sugar-free. Carob powder has a much lower fat content than cocoa.

Put the dates into a saucepan with the pineapple juice. Bring them to the boil and simmer them for 5 minutes; then liquidise them with the juice.

Mix together the flour, bicarbonate of soda and carob powder. Cream the butter or margarine and gradually beat in the liquidised dates. Beat in the flour mixture alternately with the eggs.

Put the mixture into a greased, 900 ml (1½ pint) pudding basin. Cover it with greased greaseproof paper and foil and tie them down securely. Lower the pudding into a saucepan of boiling water. Cover the pan and steam the pudding for 1½ hours, topping up the water when necessary. Turn the pudding on to a plate to serve.

To make the sauce, put the arrowroot into a bowl and mix in 6 tablespoons of the pineapple juice. Put the remaining pineapple juice into a saucepan and bring it to the boil. Stir in the arrowroot mixture and stir until the sauce is thick. Serve separately.

Note: half measures of ingredients may be used to make a smaller pudding, but it is not economical to make less than this.

APRICOT TART

Basic recipe: Shortcrust Pastry (page 87) Serves 4

Preparation time: 40 minutes + 30 minutes chilling

shortcrust pastry made with 175 g (6 oz) wholemeal flour

175 g (6 oz) curd cheese

25 g (1 oz) ground almonds

1 tablespoon honey

411 g (14½ oz) can of apricots in natural juice

6 tablespoons no-sugar-added apricot jam

Oven temperature:
Gas Mark 6/200°C/400°F

This tart is easy and inexpensive to make, but looks and tastes superb, and is therefore suitable for dinner parties as well as everyday meals.

Preheat the oven. Roll out the pastry and use it to line a 20 cm (8-inch) diameter tart tin. Line the tin with a circle of greaseproof paper or foil and fill it with dried beans or pearl barley. Bake blind for 10 minutes and then remove the paper and beans. Return the shell to the oven for a further 5–10 minutes or until it is crisp and just beginning to brown. Cool the shell in the tin and then carefully transfer it to a flat plate.

Cream the cheese in a bowl and beat in the almonds and honey. Spread the mixture in the pastry case. Drain the apricots, saving the juice to dilute and use as a drink, and put them on top of the cheese.

Put the jam into a saucepan and melt it on a low heat; then sieve it. Brush it thickly over the apricots to cover them completely. Leave the tart for 30 minutes for the glaze to set.

Rhubarb and Orange Cobbler
Apricot Tart

RHUBARB AND ORANGE COBBLER

Preparation time: 15 minutes + 30 minutes cooking — Serves 4

250 g (8 oz) rhubarb

3 medium-size oranges

50 g (2 oz) sultanas

50 g (2 oz) Barbados sugar

¼ nutmeg, grated, or ¼ teaspoon ground nutmeg

For the topping:

250 g (8 oz) wholemeal flour

½ teaspoon fine sea salt

½ teaspoon bicarbonate of soda

¼ nutmeg, grated, or ¼ teaspoon ground nutmeg

50 g (2 oz) butter or vegetable margarine

50 g (2 oz) Barbados sugar

75 g (3 oz) sultanas

3–4 tablespoons water

Oven temperature:
Gas Mark 6/200°C/400°F

Rhubarb is a tart fruit and so needs a little sugar or honey. Some sweetness, however, can come from dried fruits. Cobbler toppings are made with a scone mixture and make substantial family desserts.

Preheat the oven. Chop the rhubarb. Cut the rind and pith from the oranges, cut the flesh into quarters lengthways, and thinly slice these. Mix the rhubarb, oranges, sultanas, sugar and nutmeg and put them into a large ovenproof dish such as a pie dish.

To make the topping, put the flour into a bowl with the salt, bicarbonate of soda and nutmeg and rub in the butter or margarine. Toss in the sugar and sultanas with your fingertips. Make a well in the centre and pour in the water. Mix everything to a dough.

Divide the dough into eight pieces and form each one into a flattened round. Place the dough rounds on top of the fruit. Bake the cobbler for 30 minutes or until the top has browned.

UPSIDE-DOWN BLACKBERRY AND APPLE CAKE

Preparation time: 15 minutes + 25 minutes baking

Serves 4

125 g (4 oz) butter or vegetable margarine, plus extra for greasing

150 g (5 oz) honey

125 g (4 oz) wholemeal flour

1 teaspoon baking powder

2 eggs, beaten

250 g (8 oz) fresh or frozen blackberries

2 large dessert apples, peeled, cored and chopped

Oven temperature:
Gas Mark 4/180°C/350°F

This is a light, honey-flavoured cake with a moist topping of blackberries and apples. Serve it hot or cold with cream, yogurt or creamed smatana if you wish.

Preheat the oven. Cream the butter or margarine and beat in 125 g (4 oz) of the honey. Mix the flour with the baking powder and fold it into the butter or margarine and honey, alternately with the eggs.

Grease a 20 cm (8-inch) diameter cake tin. Mix together the blackberries, apples and remaining honey. Put them into the bottom of the tin. Spoon the cake mixture on top.

Bake the cake for 25 minutes or until the top is firm and golden brown. Turn the cake on to a round, flat plate as soon as it comes out of the oven.

Note: half measures of ingredients can be used with a 16 cm (6-inch) cake tin.

SPICED PEARS

Preparation time: 10 minutes + 40 minutes cooking — Serves 4

4 large, firm Comice pears

¼ teaspoon ground cloves

¼ teaspoon ground cinnamon

150 ml (¼ pint) red grape juice

To decorate:

natural yogurt or creamed smatana

Oven temperature:
Gas Mark 4/180°C/350°F

Comice pears are sweet and juicy and so can be sweetened with grape juice without extra sugar. If only Conference pears are available, add 2 tablespoons no-sugar-added jam or honey with the grape juice.

Preheat the oven. Peel the pears, leaving them whole with the stems on. Put them into an ovenproof dish and sprinkle them with the spices. Pour in the grape juice.

Bake the pears, uncovered, for 40 minutes, or until they are tender. Serve with natural yogurt or creamed smatana spooned over the top.

Spiced Pears

BAKING

NO-SUGAR FRUIT CAKE

Preparation time: 4 hours soaking + 15–20 minutes + about 45 minutes baking

Makes a 20 cm (8-inch) cake

250 g (8 oz) dried whole apricots

300 ml (½ pint) unsweetened orange juice

250 g (8 oz) wholemeal flour

1 teaspoon bicarbonate of soda

1 teaspoon ground mixed spice

125 ml (4 fl oz) sunflower oil, plus extra for greasing

4 eggs, beaten

125 g (4 oz) raisins

125 g (4 oz) sultanas

Oven temperature:
Gas Mark 4/180°C/350°F

Although there is no sugar in the recipe, this cake is moist and delicious. It is best stored in the refrigerator, wrapped in cling film.

Put the apricots into a saucepan with the orange juice and bring them to the boil. Take them from the heat and leave them to soak for 4 hours. Drain them, reserving the juice, and then liquidise them with 125 ml (4 fl oz) of the reserved juice. Preheat the oven.

Put the flour into a mixing bowl and add the bicarbonate of soda and the mixed spice. Make a well in the centre and gradually beat in the liquidised apricots, oil and eggs. Fold in the raisins and sultanas.

Put the mixture into a well greased, 20 cm (8-inch) diameter cake tin. Bake the cake for 45 minutes or until a fine skewer stuck in the centre comes out clean. Cool the cake in the tin for 5 minutes and then turn it on to a wire rack to cool completely.

DATE AND MALT TEABREAD

Preparation time: 20 minutes + 1 hour baking Makes a 500 g (1 lb) loaf

25 g (1 oz) malt extract

150 ml (¼ pint) milk

250 g (8 oz) wholemeal flour

1 teaspoon bicarbonate of soda

¼ nutmeg, grated, or ¼ teaspoon ground nutmeg

50 g (2 oz) butter or vegetable margarine, plus extra for greasing

1 egg, beaten

125 g (4 oz) stoned dates, chopped finely

Oven temperature:
Gas Mark 4/180°C/350°F

This semi-sweet tea bread is good either plain or buttered. It can be spread with a no-sugar-added jam or peanut butter, and is also nice with cheese.

Put the malt extract and milk into a saucepan. Set them on a low heat and stir until the malt extract has melted. Cool them a little. Preheat the oven.

In a large bowl, mix together the flour, bicarbonate of soda and nutmeg. Rub in the butter or margarine. Make a well in the centre and pour in the milk mixture. Add the egg and beat with a wooden spoon to make it a smooth, dropping consistency. Fold in the dates.

Put the mixture into the prepared tin. Bake for 1 hour or until the bread is golden brown and risen and a skewer inserted in the centre comes out clean. Turn the bread on to a wire rack to cool.

SHORTCRUST PASTRY

Preparation time: 10 minutes

250 g (8 oz) wholemeal flour, plus a little extra

a pinch of fine sea salt

125 g (4 oz) soft vegetable margarine

4 tablespoons cold water

This is the all-in-one method of making wholemeal pastry. It is easier and less time-consuming than rubbing in and always gives perfect results. You can use this method in any recipe which needs shortcrust pastry; vary the quantity to suit the recipe, but keep the proportions of flour, fat and water the same.

Put the flour and salt into a bowl and make a well in the centre. Put in the margarine and water. Stir with a fork until the margarine is evenly mixed in. Bring the mixture together with your fingers. Make a ball with the dough and dust it with flour. Leave it in a cool place for 15–20 minutes.

DATE AND RAISIN BUNS

Preparation time: 40 minutes + 50 minutes proving + 20 minutes baking — Makes 12

- *25 g (1 oz) fresh yeast or 15 g (½ oz) dried yeast*
- *175 ml (6 fl oz) milk, warmed*
- *1 teaspoon honey, if using dried yeast*
- *500 g (1 lb) wholemeal flour, plus extra for kneading*
- *1 teaspoon bicarbonate of soda*
- *1 teaspoon ground mixed spice*
- *1 teaspoon fine sea salt*
- *50 g (2 oz) butter*
- *125 g (4 oz) stoned dates, chopped*
- *125 g (4 oz) raisins*
- *2 eggs, beaten*

Oven temperature:
Gas Mark 6/200°C/400°F

These little buns are rich and spicy. They can be eaten plain or spread with butter or vegetable margarine.

If you are using fresh yeast, crumble it into a bowl and pour in the milk; if dried, pour the milk into a bowl, stir in the honey and then sprinkle in the yeast. Leave the yeast in a warm place until it is frothy.

Put the flour into a mixing bowl. Add the bicarbonate of soda, mixed spice and salt and rub in the butter. Mix in the dates and raisins. Make a well in the centre and pour in the yeast mixture and the eggs. Mix everything to a dough. Turn it on to a floured board and knead it until it is smooth. Return the dough to the bowl, cover it with a clean tea towel, and leave it in a warm place for about half an hour, or until it has doubled in size.

Preheat the oven. Knead the dough again and divide it into twelve round buns. Place them on a floured baking sheet, cover them again with the tea towel and leave them in a warm place for 20 minutes or until they have almost doubled in size.

Bake the buns for 15–20 minutes or until they are brown and sound hollow when tapped. Lift them on to wire racks to cool.

Wholemeal Bread
Date and Raisin Buns

WHOLEMEAL BREAD

Preparation time: 20 minutes + 1½ hours proving + 50 minutes baking

25 g (1 oz) fresh yeast or 15 g (½ oz) dried yeast

300 ml (½ pint) warm water

1 teaspoon sugar or honey, if using dried yeast

2 teaspoons sea salt

500 g (1 lb) wholemeal flour, plus extra for kneading

oil for greasing

1 egg, beaten (optional)

Oven temperature:
Gas Mark 6/200°C/400°F

This is a good, basic recipe for wholemeal bread that is an excellent one to begin with, if you have never attempted yeast cookery before. Cracked wheat, or sesame or poppy seeds can be sprinkled over the top as decoration, if you glaze the dough with beaten egg first.

If you are using fresh yeast, crumble it into a bowl and pour in half the warm water; if dried, dissolve the sugar or honey in half the water and sprinkle in the yeast. Leave the yeast in a warm place until it is frothy. Dissolve the salt in the remaining water.

Put the flour into a bowl and make a well in the centre. Pour in the yeast mixture and mix in a little flour from the sides of the well. Pour in the salt water and mix everything to a dough. Turn the dough on to a floured work surface and knead it until it is smooth and elastic. Return it to the bowl, cover it with a clean tea cloth and leave it in a warm place for 1 hour or until it has doubled in size.

Preheat the oven. Knead the dough again. Put it either into one 1 kg (2 lb) greased loaf tin or divide it between two 500 g (1 lb) loaf tins. Put the loaves in a warm place, cover them with a cloth again and leave them until the dough has risen above the tops of the tins.

If you want, brush the dough with beaten egg to glaze it and decorate it. Bake the large loaf for 50 minutes or the smaller ones for 40 minutes. When cooked, they sound hollow when tapped. Turn them on to wire racks to cool.

Note: the dough can be shaped into one or two round loaves, or into long 'bloomers', and baked on a baking sheet for the same amount of time; or you can make small, round rolls and bake them for 20 minutes.

TASTY CHEESE SCONES

Preparation time: 20 minutes + 20 minutes baking — Makes about 20

2 teaspoons yeast extract

150 ml (1/4 pint) boiling water

500 g (1 lb) wholemeal flour, plus a little extra

1 teaspoon sea salt

1 teaspoon bicarbonate of soda

50 g (2 oz) butter or vegetable margarine

125 g (4 oz) low-fat Cheddar-type cheese, grated finely

150 g (5.29 oz) carton of natural yogurt

Oven temperature:
Gas Mark 6/200°C/400°F

These scones have a good savoury flavour with a crisp, thin crust and a soft crumb. They are best eaten on the day that they are made.

Preheat the oven. Dissolve the yeast extract in the boiling water. Cool to lukewarm.

Put the flour into a bowl with the salt and bicarbonate of soda and rub in the butter or margarine. Toss in the cheese with your fingertips. Make a well in the centre of the flour and pour in the yeast extract solution and yogurt. Mix everything to a dough and knead it lightly to an even texture.

Roll out the dough to a thickness of about 1.5 cm (5/8 inch). Stamp it into 5 cm (2-inch) diameter rounds and lay them on a floured baking sheet. Bake the scones for 20 minutes and cool them on a wire rack.

SPICED OAT BISCUITS

Preparation time: 10 minutes + 15 minutes baking — Makes 18–20

50 g (2 oz) porridge oats

75 g (3 oz) wholemeal flour, plus a little extra

1/2 teaspoon fine sea salt

1/2 teaspoon bicarbonate of soda

1/2 teaspoon ground mixed spice

75 g (3 oz) vegetable margarine, plus extra for greasing

50 g (2 oz) pear and apple spread

Oven temperature:
Gas Mark 5/190°C/375°F

The pear and apple spread used in this recipe is a rich, sweet, commercially-produced spread made by concentrating the juices of the fruits. If it is not available, honey or Barbados sugar can be used instead.

Preheat the oven and grease and flour two baking sheets. Mix together the oats, flour, salt, bicarbonate of soda and mixed spice. Cream the margarine in a bowl and beat in the pear and apple spread, a little at a time; beat in the oat mixture.

Place walnut-sized portions of the mixture on a baking sheet, leaving a space of about 5 cm (2 inches) round each one. Flatten them slightly. Bake the biscuits for 15 minutes or until they are beginning to turn golden. Leave the biscuits on the baking trays until they are cool and firm.

SUNFLOWER CLUSTERS

Preparation time: 15 minutes + 10 minutes baking — Makes 15

50 g (2 oz) sunflower seeds

125 g (4 oz) porridge oats

40 g (1½ oz) raisins

50 g (2 oz) Barbados sugar

1 tablespoon clear honey

6 tablespoons sunflower oil

To decorate:

glacé cherries

Oven temperature:
Gas Mark 6/200°C/400°F

These chewy cakes are made with a kind of flapjack mixture and look very attractive; they are a great favourite with children.

Preheat the oven. In a bowl, mix together the sunflower seeds, porridge oats and raisins. Put the sugar, honey and oil into a saucepan. Set them on a low heat and stir until the sugar has melted. Pour the mixture into the sunflower seeds and oats and stir until all the ingredients are well mixed.

Divide the mixture between 15 small paper cake cases and top with halved or quartered glacé cherries. Arrange the cakes on a baking sheet and put them into the oven for 10 minutes. Lift them on to wire racks to cool completely.

Spiced Oat Biscuits

Frosted Honey Cake

Sunflower Clusters

FROSTED HONEY CAKE

Preparation time: 20 minutes
+ about 20 minutes baking

Makes an 18 cm (7-inch) cake

175 g (6 oz) butter, softened, or vegetable margarine, plus extra for greasing

175 g (6 oz) honey

175 g (6 oz) wholemeal flour

1 teaspoon bicarbonate of soda

3 eggs, beaten

125 g (4 oz) sultanas

For the frosting:

250 g (8 oz) curd cheese

75 g (3 oz) honey

To decorate:

25 g (1 oz) walnut halves (optional)

Oven temperature:
Gas Mark 4/180°C/350°F

Honey gives this cake a distinctive flavour. The curd cheese frosting is simple to make and far lower in fats and calories than a butter icing. It is quite soft to handle, but becomes firmer if the cake is allowed to stand for a little while.

Preheat the oven and grease two 18 cm (7-inch) diameter sponge tins.

Cream the butter or margarine in a bowl. Beat in the honey. Mix the flour with the bicarbonate of soda and beat it into the butter alternately with the eggs. Fold in the sultanas and divide the mixture between the prepared cake tins. Bake the cakes for 20 minutes or until they are firm and have shrunk slightly from the sides of the tins. Cool them in the tins for 5 minutes and then turn them on to wire racks to cool.

For the frosting, beat the curd cheese with the honey. Sandwich the cakes together with half the mixture and spread the remaining mixture on top. If you wish, decorate the cake with walnut halves.

INDEX TO RECIPES

Design and layout: Ken Vail Graphic Design
Photography: Andrew Whittuck
Stylist: Bobby Baker
Food preparation for photography: Lisa Collard
Illustrations: Richard Jacobs
Typesetting: Westholme Graphics Ltd
Printed and bound by Balding & Mansell Ltd, Wisbech, Cambs